First World War
and Army of Occupation
War Diary
France, Belgium and Germany

15 DIVISION
44 Infantry Brigade
Seaforth Highlanders (Ross-shire Buffs, the Duke of Albany's)
8th Battalion
4 July 1915 - 29 February 1916

WO95/1939/1

The Naval & Military Press Ltd
www.nmarchive.com
Published in association with The National Archives

Published by

The Naval & Military Press Ltd

Unit 10 Ridgewood Industrial Park,

Uckfield, East Sussex,

TN22 5QE England

Tel: +44 (0) 1825 749494

www.naval-military-press.com

www.nmarchive.com

This diary has been reprinted in facsimile from the original. Any imperfections are inevitably reproduced and the quality may fall short of modern type and cartographic standards.

© Crown Copyright
Images reproduced by permission of The National Archives, London, England, 2015.

Contents

Document type	Place/Title	Date From	Date To
Heading	15th Division 44th Infy Bde. 8th Bn Seaforth Hgdrs Jly 1915- Dec 1916		
Heading	July 1916 Sept 16 Appendices Are A But Difficult To Know Where They Go-Sorry.		
Heading	15th Division 8th Seaforth Highlanders Vol I July Aug & Sept. 15		
War Diary	Parkhouse Camp	04/07/1915	08/07/1915
War Diary	Boulogne	09/07/1915	09/07/1915
War Diary	Ganspette	10/07/1915	10/07/1915
War Diary	Houchin	18/07/1915	23/07/1915
War Diary	Ganspette	10/07/1915	15/07/1915
War Diary	Busnettes	16/07/1915	17/07/1915
War Diary	Houchin	24/07/1915	28/07/1915
Miscellaneous	Subject. 8th Seaforths. August. 1915.		
War Diary	Houchin	29/07/1915	01/08/1915
War Diary	South Maroc	02/08/1915	06/08/1915
War Diary	Sector W	06/08/1915	10/08/1915
War Diary	General		
War Diary	Mazingarbe	11/08/1915	16/08/1915
War Diary	Philosophe	17/08/1915	17/08/1915
War Diary	Sub-Sector XI.	18/08/1915	26/08/1915
War Diary	Philosophe	27/08/1915	29/08/1915
War Diary	Le Philosophe	30/08/1915	31/08/1915
Heading	44th Inf. Bde. 15th Div. War Diary 8th Battn. The Seaforth Highlanders. September 1915		
Miscellaneous	Report On Operations 25th September.		
Miscellaneous	From Inf. 8th Seaforth Hdrs. To Headquarters 44th Inf. Bde.	21/09/1915	21/09/1915
Miscellaneous	War Diary.		
War Diary	Noeux-Les-Mines	01/09/1915	19/09/1915
War Diary	Grenay Vermelles Main Line.	20/09/1915	25/09/1915
War Diary	Vermelles Grenay Line	26/09/1915	26/09/1915
War Diary	Malingarbe	27/09/1915	28/09/1915
War Diary	Houchin	29/09/1915	01/10/1915
War Diary		15/07/1915	19/09/1915
Miscellaneous	Battalion Operation Order No. 1.		
Operation(al) Order(s)	Operation Order No. 1. By Lieut. Col. N.A. Thomson. Commanding 8th Seaforth Highlanders. 22-9-15	22/09/1915	22/09/1915
Operation(al) Order(s)	Operation Order No. 1. By Lieut. Col. N.A. Thomson. Commanding 8th Batt. Seaforth Highlanders. 22/9/15	22/09/1915	22/09/1915
Heading	8th Seaforths October 1915		
War Diary	Houchin	01/10/1915	03/10/1915
War Diary	Lillers	05/10/1915	13/11/1915
War Diary	Noeux-Les-Mines	13/10/1915	26/10/1915
War Diary	Trenches C.2.	26/10/1915	26/10/1915
War Diary	C.2.	26/10/1915	31/10/1915
Heading	8th Seaforths. November 1915.		
War Diary	Sector C 2	01/11/1915	01/11/1915
War Diary	C 2	02/11/1915	04/11/1915
War Diary	Sector C 2	04/11/1915	04/11/1915

War Diary	C 2	04/11/1915	07/11/1915
War Diary	Noeux-Les-Mines	08/11/1915	12/11/1915
War Diary	D I.	13/11/1915	15/11/1915
War Diary	Noyelles	16/11/1915	18/11/1915
War Diary	D 1	19/11/1915	22/11/1915
War Diary	Vermelles	23/11/1915	23/11/1915
War Diary	Vermelles Verquin	24/11/1915	24/11/1915
War Diary	Verquin	24/11/1915	29/11/1915
Heading	8th Seaforths. December 1915		
War Diary	Verquin	30/11/1915	30/11/1915
War Diary	Verquin Vermelles	01/12/1915	04/12/1915
War Diary	D 1	04/12/1915	06/12/1915
War Diary	Noyelles	07/12/1915	10/12/1915
War Diary	D 1	11/12/1915	13/12/1915
War Diary	D 1 Allouagne	14/12/1915	14/12/1915
War Diary	Allouagne	14/12/1915	31/12/1915
Map	46th Brigade.		
War Diary	Allouagne	01/01/1916	05/01/1916
War Diary	Rely	06/01/1916	07/01/1916
War Diary	Allouagne	08/01/1916	14/01/1916
War Diary	Poits 14 Bis Sector	15/01/1916	20/01/1916
War Diary	Tenth Avenue	21/01/1916	23/01/1916
Diagram etc	A Coy		
War Diary	Right Sub-Section-Puits XIV Bis Section	24/01/1916	25/01/1916
War Diary	Right Sub-Section	26/01/1916	26/01/1916
War Diary	Noeux-Les-Mines	27/01/1916	01/02/1916
War Diary	Trenches	02/02/1916	10/02/1916
War Diary	Philosophe	11/02/1916	19/02/1916
Diagram etc	Sub-Section, Poits XIV Bis Section.		
War Diary	Trenches	20/02/1916	29/02/1916

15TH DIVISION
44TH INFY BDE

8TH BN SEAFORTH HGDRS
JLY 1915 - DEC 1916

July 1916 } Appendices are a bit difficult to know where they go - guess -
Sept 16

I.W.
7 sheets

8th Seaforths
July 1915.

8th Seaforth Highlanders.

Vol: I

July Aug & Sept 15

WAR DIARY
or
INTELLIGENCE SUMMARY.
(Erase heading not required.)

Army Form C. 2118.

of 8th (Service) Bn.
SEAFORTH HIGHLANDERS

Place	Date	Hour	Summary of Events and Information	Remarks and references to Appendices
PARKHOUSE CAMP	4/7/15	10.45am	Opr. order was this day received from Headquarters 44th I.B. warning the Bn. to be ready to proceed overseas. Capt G.R. ANDERSON was sent over to France to perform disembarking duties for 15th Division.	
	6/7/15		Mobilization was this day completed, the strength of the Bn. being 31 officers (including Medical Officer and Chaplain) and 983 other ranks. List of officers is as follows:—	

1. Command Lt-Col N.A. THOMSON
Major 2nd in Command { SWINBURNE U.F.
Major { TREMEARNE A.I.H.
Officers   MUNRO H.F.
           POWELL R.M.
           RAVENHILL A.G.
           MURRAY G.
           FORSYTH C.C.
           ANDERSON G.R.
           MYES J.F.
           DUNLOP D.M.
Lieutenants

Lts. STANFORD T.V.
      HOLMES F.
      FERGUSSON F.K.O.
      KENNEDY J.E.
      MACAULAY D.S.
      DUNCAN G.W.
      MILLAR R.C.
2/Lts PAYNE J.R.S.
      TURNBULL A.W.
      GEORGESON D.H.
      TREMEARNE W.C.

MACGREGOR G.
CALDER G.T.
NICHOLSON J.M.L.
MACRAE F.L.
HEATH W.

ADJUTANT
CAPT. D.W.P. STRANG
QUARTERMASTER
LT. A R. JEFFREY
MEDICAL OFFICER
LT. E. ROBINSON
CHAPLAIN
CAPT. W. CRAWFORD

WAR DIARY
or
INTELLIGENCE SUMMARY

Army Form C. 2118.

Place	Date	Hour	Summary of Events and Information	Remarks and references to Appendices
PARKHOUSE CAMP	7/7/15	8.15 a.m.	Details, consisting of Transport Section, M.G. Section, Signal Section, Staff Personnel under Major U/P Swinburne left Tidworth Station to proceed to Southampton. Hence to Havre. The party numbered 3 officers (Major Swinburne, Lt. Col. Duncan, Transport Officer, M.T. N.C. Trembarne M.G.O.) and 97 N.C.O.s and men. Motor transport cycles M.Guns and horses, ammunition accompanied the party.	
	8/7/15	3.10 p.m.	"A" & "B" Coys under the C.O. left Tidworth Station for FOLKESTONE Hence to BOULOGNE.	
BOULOGNE	9/7/15	4.53 p.m.	"C" & "D" Coys under O.C. "D" Coy (Major A.S.H. Trembarne) followed	
		10.50 a.m.	"A" & "B" Coys under the C.O. arrived at Ostrohove Rest Camp Boulogne.	
		2.30 a.m.	"C" & "D" under O.C. "D" Coy arrived	
		10.15 p.m.	The Battalion, less details, left OSTROHOVE REST CAMP and marched to PONT DE BRIQUES Station where it entrained. Having regained sufficiently, advanced party under Major U/P Swinburne.	
		5 p.m.	Battalion arrived at WATTEN and detrained. The Battalion proceeded to GANSPETTE where it took up billets.	
GANSPETTE	10/7/15		Battalion remained rather the billeting area for the day. The fields	

WAR DIARY
or
INTELLIGENCE SUMMARY.
(Erase heading not required.)

Army Form C. 2118.

(4)

Instructions regarding War Diaries and Intelligence Summaries are contained in F.S. Regs, Part II. and the Staff Manual respectively. Title pages will be prepared in manuscript.

Place	Date	Hour	Summary of Events and Information	Remarks and references to Appendices
HOUCHIN	18/7/15	—	FOUQUEREIL – E of FOUQUIERES – VAUDRICOURT to HOUCHIN, where it went into billets. DWF	
			The Bn. remained in billeting area, cleaning up billets, which were found in a very dirty condition. DWF A+B Coys left for 2 days rest to trenches W8	
	19/7/15		Bn. remained in billeting area. C.O. Adj. +5 warrant officers left to visit trenches between DWF	
	20/7/15		Bn remained in billeting area: the Brigade billeting area being as follows:—	
			Reference 40,000 sheet 36 b Square K:—	
			N. Road Junction 9.a. Central – 10.a.10.5	
			E. Road Junction 10.a.10.5 – x-roads 16.a.9.9 – x-roads 16.c.8.6	
			S. x-roads 16.c.8.6 – x-roads 15.D.3.9 – x-roads 15.a.2.1	
			W. x-roads 15.a.2.1 – Road Junction 9.a. Central.	
			Bn. dug shelters in case of German retaliatory shelling on billets. DWF	
	21/7/15		Bn. remained in billeting area. Intrenching continued. DWF	
	22/7/15		Bn remained in billeting area. C & D Coys left on a tour of inspection of trenches. DWF	
	23/7/15		Bn remained in billeting area. Machine gun unit was increased this day to 3 officers and 72 men – viz (1) (2) and (3) sections, the	

WAR DIARY
or
INTELLIGENCE SUMMARY.

Army Form C. 2118.
(3)

Place	Date	Hour	Summary of Events and Information	Remarks and references to Appendices
GANSPETTE	10/7/15	—	were on the whole good. Training was carried on under Coy. arrangements	Staff
"	11/7/15	—	Battalion remained within the Billeting Area. Training under Coy. arrangements	Staff
"	12/7/15	—	The Battalion marched out, in order of march "B" Coy, "C", "D", "A". Reference Route, x-roads 200 yds S. & first E of PERLECQUES – 1st A of LA CALIFORNIE – O of BLANCHE – ROUGE – MILL, ½ mile N. G of RUMINGHEM – across the railway line at LE QUILLEVAL – WATTEN – GANSPETTE. Training was carried on under Coy. arrangements within the billeting-area, with special attention to FIRE DIRECTION and FIRE CONTROL.	Staff
"	13/7/15	—		
"	14/7/15	—	The Battalion paraded for Coy. marches within the Brigade Billeting Area; Signal and M.G. sections training independently.	Staff
"	15/7/15	—	The Battn. left GANSPETTE at 6.10 a.m, and marched to HAZEBROUCK, where it billeted for the night.	Staff
BUSNETTES	16/7/15	—	The Battn left HAZEBROUCK at 8.10 a.m, and marched to BUSNETTES where it billeted for the night.	Staff
"	17/7/15	—	The Battn left BUSNETTES at 8.20 p.m, and marched via CHOCQUES,	

WAR DIARY
or
INTELLIGENCE SUMMARY.
(Erase heading not required.)

Army Form C. 2118.

Place	Date	Hour	Summary of Events and Information	Remarks and references to Appendices
HOUCHIN	24/7/15	—	Officers being respectively 2/Lt W.C. TREMEARNE, Lt F HOLMES & Lt. D. B. MACAULAY. No (1) and (2) sections are brigaded under Brigade M.G. Officer. No (3) Section, a second reserve section, will remain with their Bn.	DwBy
"	25/7/15	—	Bn. remained in billeting area :-	DwBy
"	26/7/15	—	Bn. remained in billeting area.	
			Bn. route-marched by Coy; in the area W. of HOUCHIN – BARLIN. All men of the Transport Section, M.G. sections, Signalling sections, officers' servants and servants located at Bn. Headquarters with men on staff employment were this day formed into a new Headquarters unit to be called "R" Coy, under Major N.P. SWINBURNE, with the Bn. Sgt. Major as Senior N.C.O. — The unit to be for purpose of clothing, rations, and transport, men continuing to draw their pay from their original Coys.	DwBy DwBy
"	27/7/15	—	Bn. remained in billeting area :- Coy. & Specialist Training	DwBy
"	28/7/15	—	Bn. remained in billeting area :- Coy. & Specialist Training	DwB3

Index..........

SUBJECT.
8th Seaforths

2.W
15 attack

No.	Contents.	Date.
	August 1915.	

WAR DIARY
or
INTELLIGENCE SUMMARY.
(Erase heading not required.)

Army Form C. 2118.

Place	Date	Hour	Summary of Events and Information	Remarks and references to Appendices
HOUCHIN	29/7/15		Bn. route-marched in Coy. within Bn. safety-area. "K" Coy inflected. Coy. Runners organised (2 per Coy) for rumour work in the trenches.	DNP
"	30/7/15		Bn. remained in billeting area :- Specialist Coy training - specially practice in the charging and unloading of magazines.	DNP
"	31/7/15		Bn. remained in billeting area :- training as on previous day.	DNP
"	1/8/15	8.30 p.m.	The Bn. passed HOUCHIN Church 4 minutes interval between companies, en route for MAROC to take over billets from the 17th LONDON REGT., as Battalion in Brigade Reserve in Sector W1. of the line. Relief was completed about midnight.	DNP
SOUTH MAROC	2/8/15		Brigade Provisional Defence for Sector W received. Provisional Defence Scheme for Bn. in Brigade Reserve issued by the Commanding Officer.	DNP
	3/8/15		Bn. remained under cover about billets to prevent attracting enemy's artillery. Working party of 290 men worked during night on improvement of trenches mainly in sector W 3.	DNP
	4/8/15		Sector quiet. Working party of 450 men provided for work in W at night.	DNP
	5/8/15		Sector quiet. Working party of 500 men furnished for work in W during night.	DNP
	6/8/15		This day and night 3rd Seaforth Highrs. took over sub-sector W1. from 7	

Army Form C. 2118.

WAR DIARY
or
INTELLIGENCE SUMMARY.
(Erase heading not required.)

Place	Date	Hour	Summary of Events and Information	Remarks and references to Appendices
SECTOR W1	6/8/15		Ameer Hilpho Headquarters documents and Trench Stores in So. MAROC were taken over during the afternoon: relief of the trenches commenced at 8.30 p.m.: Completed about 11 p.m. Dispositions of Coys were as follows: 1 Fire Trench { Right — "B" Coy { Left — "C" Coy 2. Supports — "A" Coy 3 Reserve — "D" Coy 4 Headquarters — Billets in So. MAROC.	The first casualties (seven enquires) this day viz 5/63rd Battalion W1 Coy Cecil Nicholson shot in the scalp and in the side of the nose by shrapnel splinter.
"	7/8/15		SITUATION QUIET.	
"	8/8/15		SITUATION QUIET	
" +	9/8/15		SITUATION QUIET. Five Inf. "Guards" came into Negro Redoubt, one of what came into the Redoubt without Lotching anyone.	
"	10/8/15		Battalion relieved in Sector W1 by 7th K.O.S.B. Relief carried out by right, commencing about 9.30 p.m. The relief was completed without incident by about 11.30 p.m. The 9th Leinpth Hilpho pro- ceeded to MAZINGARBE and took over billets of the K.O.S.Border ers.	

1577 Wt. W10791/1773 500,000 1/15 D. D. & L. A.D.S.S./Forms/C. 2118.

Army Form C. 2118.

WAR DIARY
or
INTELLIGENCE SUMMARY
(Erase heading not required.)

Instructions regarding War Diaries and Intelligence Summaries are contained in F. S. Regs., Part II. and the Staff Manual respectively. Title pages will be prepared in manuscript.

Place	Date	Hour	Summary of Events and Information	Remarks and references to Appendices
GENERAL			INFORMATION REGARDING W.1.	

This section of the line has been very quiet. Activity was mainly confined on the Enemy's side and ours to firing from trench mortars. No 9 French Mortar Battery was operating in our sector; and on one occasion seemed to silence an Enemy battery — a success which brought over one Enemy shrapnel. Otherwise the Enemy did not shell our trenches, except for the few "strafes" mentioned did not shell billets in MAROC. This may have been explained by the fact that our artillery, apart from registering the first day, was not active during the period. The Enemy shelled (fairly regularly) Rows 5 and 11, N.E. & S.W. of MAROC respectively.

With regard to the interior Economy of the Battalion the greatest difficulties experience were with cooking and the supply of water.

(a) Cooking had to be done in the railway-cutting between N. & S. MAROC over a mile from the front trenches. This involves large fatigues everyday lessening the number of Rifles immediately available at extreme times during the day to man the trenches in case of attack. These fatigues

WAR DIARY
or
INTELLIGENCE SUMMARY.
(Erase heading not required.)

Army Form C. 2118.

Place	Date	Hour	Summary of Events and Information	Remarks and references to Appendices
			which themselves alone involved 80 men being about from the trenches three times daily, could be largely avoided if cooking were done in the trenches.	
			(b) The Water-Supply presented a similar difficulty — large fatigues being necessary to carry water from check-wells N of the railway — looking into the trenches. This difficulty it seems could be easily obviated by running a pipe into the trenches.	
			Mining operations on the part of the Enemy were suspected in this sector. A careful examination was made of the neighbouring mines through Brigade Headquarters; and counter-mining was begun in the front trench.	
			A considerable amount of heavy sniping was reported, and some was believed to have taken place from the village of MAROC itself. Careful patrolling was instituted, but as there are some 500 or 600 unoccupied houses in the neighbourhood it appears some 30 men would be necessary for the duty.	
			D.W.P.S.	

Army Form C. 2118.

WAR DIARY
or
INTELLIGENCE SUMMARY.
(Erase heading not required.)

Instructions regarding War Diaries and Intelligence Summaries are contained in F.S. Regs., Part II. and the Staff Manual respectively. Title pages will be prepared in manuscript.

Place	Date	Hour	Summary of Events and Information	Remarks and references to Appendices
MAZINGARBE	11/8/15		The Battalion is now in Divisional Reserve. Coy. military operation carried on work on the line of defence GRENAY — VERMELLES under direction of the 74th Field Coy. R.E. — Working party of 5 officers and 300 men reported at 7.45 p.m. this day to R.E.	Dr.ft.
	12/8/15		No incident	
	13/8/15		Working party of 5 officers and 300 men found as on 11/8/15	Dr.ft.
	14/8/15		No incident	
	15/8/15		Working party of 6 officers and 300 men found as on 11/8/15, 13/8/15	Dr.ft.
	16/8/15		No incident	
PHILOSOPHE	17/8/15		The Batt. left MAZINGARBE (to platoons at 4 minutes interval, "C" Coy leading) proceeding to PHILOSOPHE. Billets taken over from 13th Royal Scots.	
SUB-SECTOR X.1	18/8/15		Battalion left PHILOSOPHE (in order B, D, C, A, & Coys) to take over Section X.1 of the line from the 7th Royal Scots Fusiliers. The relief was effected during the afternoon without incident. Notice having this day reached that Cpl. F. MYLES was wounded in England the trenches at 15 minutes interval.	Dr.ft.
"	19/8/15		X.1. Battalion was distributed as follows :—	

1577 Wt. W10791/1773 500,000 1/15 D. D. & L. A.D.S.S./Forms/C. 2118.

WAR DIARY
or
INTELLIGENCE SUMMARY.
(Erase heading not required.)

Army Form C. 2118.

(11)

Place	Date	Hour	Summary of Events and Information	Remarks and references to Appendices

Three Coys in the firing line in trenches, one Company in reserve in QUALITY STREET. The Coys in the firing line were:—

RIGHT. "B" COY on the right, 2 Platoons in the firing line, 1 Platoon in support, 1 Platoon in QUALITY KEEP SOUTH.

CENTRE "C" COY, three Platoons in the firing line, 1 Platoon in support.

LEFT "D" COY, two Platoons in the firing line, one Platoon in support, and one in the QUALITY KEEP EAST.

To-day the dispositions were changed. The Platoons in the keeps were sent forward to the support line of their respective companies; and a half Platoon was put in each Keep from the reserve Company (A).

To-day all the machine Guns of the Battalion were brought into the sector. On the 15th inst, three had been sent up to the Trenches being attached to the 75th I.B.; lately the control of the Machine Gun Sections Partly by the Brigade, partly by the Battalion led, from the cause of some difficulty — alike from the point of view of discipline and training, and of tactical handling. The guns are now brought into the area in the life

WAR DIARY
or
INTELLIGENCE SUMMARY
(Erase heading not required.)

Army Form C. 2118.

Place	Date	Hour	Summary of Events and Information	Remarks and references to Appendices
			of getting greater battalion control. The Brigade Machine Gun Officer is to take the role of expert tactical adviser. It would be better if the guns were taken over entirely by the Brigade, (as a special corps) or left entirely to the battalion. The peculiar conditions of trench warfare perhaps, make the latter course impracticable. The machine guns are needed in the trenches of the battalion they have been attached to, and the fact this removes them from battalion control. The fact that guns are thus constantly detached from the units to which they belong, and are handled practically as a separate arm, points to the nominally and in the near future a special corps afforded for purpose use by their learning and of tactical handling. firstly of tactical machine and discipline.	
	19/8/15		For 24 hours ending 12 noon enemy artillery was on the whole quiet. There was some sniping especially on the left; where along our front mortar bombs fell between the FIRE TRENCH and the SUPPORT trench at 10.40 P.M. 2 enemy movement target of 4 men on the left was shelled during the period. There was little activity on our part; the artillery was quiet, and there was only occasional rifle-firing at enemy snipers etc.	

WAR DIARY
or
INTELLIGENCE SUMMARY.

Army Form C. 2118.

(3)

Place	Date	Hour	Summary of Events and Information	Remarks and references to Appendices
Sub-Sector X.1.	2/8/15	12 noon	Owing to the friable nature of the soil, the condition of the trenches is not good. The sides of the trenches constantly fall in at places. The trenches are shallow in many places; the parapets and parados partly constructed; and traversing, fire-stepping, provision of dug-out accommodation is incomplete. A scheme of dug-out accommodation is in course of construction by the O.C. London Regts. (Reserve). This, on the other hand, retards the trenches very considerably. As the number of men working thickens the nuage, and also the sandbags which are filled during the day to be supplied at night, and the putt[...]s and other material necessary to the construction of dug-outs. The work of recently erected proceeds very slowly. S.T.W.P.J. During this 24 hours there has been no enemy shelling. Enemy snipers were fairly active. On our side rifle firing was intermittent in reply to enemy snipers. Two trench mortar shells were flung over to the enemy trenches on the night of the LENS road, retaliatory for 3 shells flung from the German lines (which, however, did no damage.) S.T.W.P.J.	I have recorded during this period — though feint which in habit from hoplites [?]
	3/8/15	12 noon	During this period the enemy threw over about 30 shells on the	

WAR DIARY
or
INTELLIGENCE SUMMARY

Army Form C. 2118.

(14)

Place	Date	Hour	Summary of Events and Information	Remarks and references to Appendices
Sub Section N	12/9/15	13 noon	Fire and support trenches. Sniping was fairly active. Enemy working parties were out during dark, apparently repairing parapet wires on our side. There was little activity, but a good deal of work was done deepening the trenches, repairing parapets and putting up wire platforms. 20 last rounds fuses were driven in and iron rods with hanger- and groove flanking. Casualty list — 1 man very slight wounded with shaped splinter in the face. Draft of 1 offr, 31 nco's and 27 men arrived this day P.m.P. Enemy sent out during time scouts came to stella. Sniping was fairly active on the left coy. Enemy wire parties working during the night repairing their parapets to the N of the LENS road. Working parties were also seen apparently working on a new the J trench from G.28.C.7.6 — G.28.C 9.8 (Ref. 10,000 AUCHY — LENS map) Rifle fire on our part was negligible. Head mortar Emplacements the Artillery carried on not—registering: Batteries D7.01, D73, B.71, D73 (Heavy) Battery fired 5 rounds to silence an enemy Trench mortar battery. A working party in sight was required to repair the damage	

WAR DIARY
or
INTELLIGENCE SUMMARY
(Erase heading not required.)

Army Form C. 2118.

Place	Date	Hour	Summary of Events and Information	Remarks and references to Appendices
Sd Sector X1	23/8/15	noon	Work was continued as yesterday, repairing trenches — deepening, revetting parapet and traverses, fire steps, improving dug-out accommodation. DSTJ During the period there was occasional shelling of the trenches. Sniping was more active than hitherto. Enemy working parties were very active at a work of some importance in the neighbourhood of the LENS road. Work was carried on in new enemy trench referred to yesterday. On our front there was slight rifle firing on enemy working parties but French mortar Battery at 2 a.m. Although continually harassing enemy working party, Sabots sent out from all CoyS but movement was hindered by clear moonlight. There was no C.G. Garden between our party and artillery during the period.	This day the first German letter was brought to the regiment by a Police Pte No 3144 Pte T. MORRISON and was refused about the position of PS with the efforts trenches about noon DSTJ
"	24/8/15	noon	Work was continued, as during yesterday. It was repairing trenches. This was the most active period so far for the enemy's artillery. The shelling first before noon on the trenches day was kept up intermittently during the period. The firing which was heaviest about noon on the 23(?)	DSTJ

WAR DIARY or INTELLIGENCE SUMMARY

Army Form C. 2118.

(16)

Place	Date	Hour	Summary of Events and Information	Remarks and references to Appendices
Sec section N1	28/8/15		was direct at the Front, Support and Communication trenches of the Centre and Left Coys. The only casualty was the Artist - Private reported yesterday. Sniping was markedly increased on the Left Coy, above about a dozen rifle grenades also came over, but was as usual with other 2" Coys. Working parties were started from Sep 16, and also on new German trench referred to on 22nd and 23rd. There was some rifle-firing on our side at working parties the during the night. A reply to ± 12 inch shells that enemy threw over and do activity of enemy artillery D 73 battery put about a dozen shells on the Army front line trenches at G 25 B. 3.'s and in the vicinity of the LENS Road. At the latter place bits and working material were seen to fly in the air. Work was carried on repairing, revetting, fire-stepping, improving trenches etc. 8 yds of trench had to be cleared by the Left Coy near the furthest fell in and filled the trench to a depth of 3 feet. About 20 shells came over during the forenoon — on to the Left Coy.	

WAR DIARY
INTELLIGENCE SUMMARY
(Erase heading not required.)

Army Form C. 2118.

(17)

Place	Date	Hour	Summary of Events and Information	Remarks and references to Appendices
			Sniping as all was less severe. A large enemy working party was seen between 8.35 p.m. and 11.35 p.m. in the vicinity of the LENS road. Fire was so attempt at concealment, but a good deal of rumble on horseback was plainly seen. C-Operation of D 73 (H.S. and Howitzer Battery) was requested, and our shots dispersed the party for the night.	
Sub Sector X1.	18/9/15	Noon	Work was carried on in the trenches as usual. Sep 18 in particular was deepened to 10 feet over all. On the left trenches I cut the enemy put on a few shells. Our activity was on the centre. Trench mortars were active. A considerable amount of work however was done on the trenches. A considerable.	
		5 p.m.	Relief of 8th Seaforth tho. by 9th Black Watch in Sub Sector X1 commenced. "D" Coy. 8th Seaforth tho. remaining in the line from Bryan 8.B. (Frelinhein) to Bryan 9a (inclusive) to allow of rearrangement in the division of the front between divisions. Machine Gun	

Army Form C. 2118.

WAR DIARY
or
INTELLIGENCE SUMMARY.
(Erase heading not required.)

Instructions regarding War Diaries and Intelligence Summaries are contained in F.S. Regs., Part II. and the Staff Manual respectively. Title pages will be prepared in manuscript.

Place	Date	Hour	Summary of Events and Information	Remarks and references to Appendices
PHILOSOPHE	27/8/15		detachments also remained in the line. The 8th Seaforth Hrs. (less D Coy. and M.G. Section) took over billets from 7th Cameron Hrs. in LE PHILOSOPHE, where they came into Brigade Reserve. D.W.P.J. Battalion remained in billets, cleaning these up. These billets, as reported by the Medical Officer to A.D.M.S. 15th Divsn were in a filthy condition. Working Party of 200 men furnished for constructing a bombing course at Brigade Headquarters. Party reported to Bde. Headquarters at 1.30 p.m. "D" Coy. 8th Seaforth Hrs. was relieved at Sector X.1 at 4 p.m. and rejoined the battalion. D.W.P.J. "B" & "C" Coys. reported for work to R.E. party. 5 Officers and 200 men employed Constructing Reserve Trenches in X.1 sector. D.W.P.J.	
"	28/8/15	8 p.m.	Battalion remained in billets. Working Party of 8 officers and 400 men under Capt. A.G. Rainsheff at 8 p.m. m... Work in Reserve Trenches X.1. D.W.P.J.	
"	29/8/15		Battalion remained in billets.	

WAR DIARY
or
INTELLIGENCE SUMMARY.
(Erase heading not required.)

Army Form C. 2118.

Place	Date	Hour	Summary of Events and Information	Remarks and references to Appendices

---

WAR DIARY
or
INTELLIGENCE SUMMARY.
(Erase heading not required.)

Army Form C. 2118.

Place	Date	Hour	Summary of Events and Information	Remarks and references to Appendices
LE PHILOSOPHE	3/9/15	8pm	Working party reported to Advanced R.E. Store. 8 Officers 400 men under Capt R.M. POWELL. Work on Reserve Trenches X.1.	
		6.45pm	Battalion left LE PHILOSOPHE and marched in order "A", "B", "C", "D" "K" Coys to NOEUX-LES-MINES, where it took over billets from the 13th ROYAL SCOTS, and went with the Brigade into Divisional Reserve.	
	3/9/15		Battalion remained in billets. Working party of 2 Officers and 120 men to R.E. Dump	

44th Inf.Bde.
15th Div.

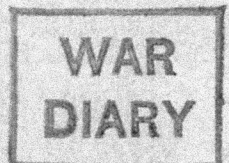

8th BATTN. THE SEAFORTH HIGHLANDERS.

SEPTEMBER

1915

Attached:
Report On Ops. 25.9.15.
Battalion O.O. No. 1.

REPORT ON OPERATIONS 25TH SEPTEMBER.

From O.C. 8th Seaforth Hdrs
To Headquarters 44th Inf Bde.

As Senior Officer left after the attack of the 8th Seaforth as part of the 44th Brigade on the German position on 25th inst. I have the honour to submit the following report:—

On notification that Zero hour was 5.50 a.m. Lt-Col N.C. THOMPSON ordered all men to stand to arms at 5 a.m. with smoke helmet on ready for use. At 5.50 a.m. gas discharge commenced under fairly favourable conditions. Whether however it was due to the bursting of a cylinder or the nature of the wind a considerable number of the leading Coy of the battalion suffered from the effects of gas before leaving the trenches. The smoke candles were exceedingly effective and promptly to the minute "A" Coy of the

②

8th Seaforth Hrs. leaped the parapet, "B", "C" & "D" coys following in quick succession.

The German wire was well cut by our Artillery, and the losses which we had here were not due to delay caused by the wire so much as to the very heavy artillery and machine gun fire of the enemy. The losses were disastrous to the battalion with regard to the Senior Officers. The Colonel and Second in Command who had gone over the parapet well forward were left not far from our own trenches, and the four Coy Commanders were in similar case. I did not realise that by this time I was in command of the regiment. Although seeing the second-in-command down and having lost touch with the Colonel I forthwith proceed to endeavour to communicate with the Brigade.

The central street of Loos running E and W was taken as the

right of the line of advance of the 8th Seaforth Adrs & making for there. However, we again suffered heavily owing to strong German Machine Gun positions on the edge of the town. Bombers were pushed into the town, and did excellent work, the remainder of the battalion keeping more to the left and pushing on quickly. Owing to the rapid advance touch was lost somewhat, I think, with the Brigade on the left.

Beyond Loos the battalions of the Brigade had become considerably mixed up together: and there seemed to be no officer of the Brigade beyond the rank of Captain in the front line.

In advancing the village of Loos and the crassiers behind the pylons seemed to increase a bad preservation on the firing line. The line also was probably inclined to the right by the desire to get touch with the London Division.

The result was that the Seaforth

④

Hrs. and Black Watch mixed up with Gordons and Camerons left the German work at H 31 Central on their left and advanced on the CITÉ ST LAURENT rather than the CITÉ AUGUSTE. The right of the line emerged directly on PUITS 12, where no further advance was impossible owing to the fact that our heavy artillery was shelling the mine, and apparently searching for a battery right up against which we had arrived, and which continued to fire in our immediate neighbourhood until one gun was knocked out by one of our shells.

As advance was obviously impossible here the line then inclined to the left and directed its attack against a position extending from PUITS 12 to the DYNAMITIÈRE at H.1.B.1.2. The Dynamitière was strongly held by Machine guns and our guns began wasting their ammunition

⑤

at the point. This seemed to check the line, for after an hr it apparently wavered. I had retired to the top of the hill to attempt an appreciation of the situation; and when I got to the Keep, found there a young Engineer, Lt Johnstone, who instantly convinced me of the necessity of rallying the men there and holding the hill on this line. We failed to induce the men to remain in the Keep; but succeeded in making them hold on to a bank on which the whole line subsequently retired; and getting the fire under control we were able to hold up the German counter attack. It certainly looked for the moment as if our whole offensive was going to be swept off the hill; and I think it was due entirely to the judgment of the young Engineer that the situation was saved.

Colonel Wallace of the Gordons

(6)

Then started forming a line behind and lower down on which I understand he was later joined by Lt Col. Sandilands.

Hearing the Brigade was at Loos I proceeded there to state the situation. After explaining the position which I was holding with a mixed collection of men from different arrangements I was on taken I would be relieved and authorised to withdraw what remained of the 8th Seaforth Hdrs. when Lt Col Jackson of the R.Royal Scots had consolidated the position on the hill.

This was done during the night and I withdrew the 8th Seaforth Hdrs. one day officer myself and 135 NCOs & Rank & file to the VERMELLES- GRENAY line of defence.

I have the honour to be Sir
Your obedient servant
Duncan W. P. Shang
7/9/15   Capt & Adjt
8th Seaforth Hdrs.

WAR DIARY.

Army Form C. 2118.

P 19

WAR DIARY
or
INTELLIGENCE SUMMARY.

8/Seaforth Highlanders.

(Erase heading not required.)

Title pages September 1915.

Place	Date	Hour	Summary of Events and Information	Remarks and references to Appendices
[NOEUX-LES-MINES]	1/9/15		Battalion in billets. Working party of 4 officers and 300 men under Major A.J.N. TREMEARNE returned to R.E.I. (91st Fd Cy) at MAZINGARBE. 7.45p.m. Duty.	
	2/9/15		Battalion in billets. Night working party to R.E at MAZINGARBE of 3 officers and 140 men under Capt. E.P. MURRAY. Duty.	
	3/9/15		Battalion in billets. Night working party of 2 officers and 130 men under Capt. C.C. FORSYTH to R.E at MAZINGARBE. Duty.	
	4/9/15		Battalion in billets. Night working party of 4 officers and 190 men to R.E. at MAZINGARBE under Capt. G.R. ANDERSON D.V. R.I.	
	5/9/15		Battalion in billets. Night working party of 3 officers and 140 men to R.E. at MAZINGARBE under Capt. A.G. RAVENHILL.	

WAR DIARY
or
INTELLIGENCE SUMMARY.

(Erase heading not required.)

Army Form C. 2118.

Place	Date	Hour	Summary of Events and Information	Remarks and references to Appendices
NOEUX-LES-MINES	6/9/15		Lt. & 2nd Lt. A.R. JEFFREY evacuated owing to eye trouble to H.Q. 11th F.A. Battalion brought 7 Sgt. 2 Cpls. 145 ptes. arrived this day. 300 men under Capt. G. MURRAT in billets. Working party of 6 officers and R.E. at MAZINGARBE at 6.30 p.m. draft	(2)
	7/9/15 4 p.m.		G. MURRAT refused to go 1st FLD CY R.E at MAZINGARBE. 2nd Seaforth Hdrs. left NOEUX-LES-MINES to relieve K.A, B, C, D Coys and went into close billets at MAZINGARBE now occupied by 9th BLACK WATCH. But movement has been made in preparation for an attack on the German position. The plan of which was conveyed verbally to the C.O. draft.	
	8/9/15 4 p.m.		Battalion returned to NOEUX-LES-MINES into bivouac, nearly to move at half an hours notice. This movement has been understood to have been the attack on the German position has been postponed. To-day Battalion Bombing Course has been completed: 1 N.C.O and 7 men per Platoon having been given a 3 days' course. A little Bombing has been done at PARK HOUSE Camp before being sent to Eng- land. Training in Eng- land was on the lines more of Field Warfare than Trench Warfare, a fact due partly to the difficulty of providing material for the large new armies in training and at the same time equipping the armies in the field. The limitations imposed by circumstances in training in England are regrettable,	

WAR DIARY
INTELLIGENCE SUMMARY

Place	Date	Hour	Summary of Events and Information	Remarks and references to Appendices
NŒUX-LES-MINES	9/9/15		and have left a considerable amount to be done locally, and possibly in position imperfectly in France. It has certainly thrown considerable additional labour and strain both on Officers and men. O.T.T.U. Battalion in Billets. Working parties of 1 Officer and 25 N.C.O.s and men proceeded to MAZINGARBE at 7.45 to construct Batteries and Shelters. Two Officers proceeded to GRENAY – VERMELLES line of trenches which the Battalion will occupy during preliminary stages of artillery bombardment and for the attack on the enemy's position. During later stage of the bombardment the Battalion, according to rebel information from Bde. Headquarters, will move up to Front trenches & to form part of the Front line of assault on the German Position. O.T.T.U. Working party of 6 Officers and 300 men reported to Bde. Headquarters.	
	9/9/15		CHATEAU MAZINGARBE at 5.30 p.m.	a/6.9.15 received
	10/9/15		Battalion in billets. Working party as on 9/9/15. "Principles of Attack" 1st Army General Staff No. G.S. 164 (a) Also Att. I Inf. Bde. Notes on ATTACK No. S. 33.	

WAR DIARY
or
INTELLIGENCE SUMMARY.

(Erase heading not required.)

Army Form C. 2118.

(22)

Place	Date	Hour	Summary of Events and Information	Remarks and references to Appendices
NOEUX-LES-MINES	11/9/15		Battalion in billets. Parties continued work on GRENAY - VERMELLES line.	D.R.O.
	12/9/15		Battalion in billets. Working parties of 750 men sent up to 73rd F'ld Coy R.E. at MAZINGARBE. At 6.15pm another party of same strength at 6.30pm. Work on trenches in sector X1.	D.R.O.
"	13/9/15		Battalion in billets. Working parties as on 12/9/15. Bde. Ordr. No10 recd.	D.R.O.
"	14/9/15		Battalion in billets. Working parties as follows 100 men to 70 "B" Bde R.F.A.) 50 men to 73rd Fld Coy R.E.	D.R.O.
"	15/9/15		Battalion in billets. Working party of 150 Rand & field R.E. at QUALITY STREET at 7pm.	D.R.O.
"	16/9/15		Battalion in billets. Working party of 150 men to 73rd Fld Coy R.E at MAZINGARBE at 6.15pm. "A" Coy in field trying Enemy Gent Pickmen(?) in attack order. Similar party at 3.30pm.	D.R.O.
"	17/9/15		Battalion in billets. 300 men reported to R.E. store at QUALITY STREET in two parties at 6.45pm and 7pm respectively.	D.R.O.
	18/9/15		Battalion in billets. Working party of 150 men to 73rd Fld Coy R.E. at 6.30pm.	D.R.O.
NOEUX-LES-MINES	19/9/15	5pm	Battalion left NOEUX-LES-MINES in order K, A, B, C, D Coys for GRENAY-	

WAR DIARY
INTELLIGENCE SUMMARY

(23)

Place	Date	Hour	Summary of Events and Information	Remarks and references to Appendices
GRENAY VER- MELLES main line	24/9/15	9.30 a.m.	VERMELLES Main line of trenches. Notification received that 2/Lt. & 2nd Lt. A.R. JEFFREY was unable to proceed to England. Brigade Operation Order No 12 (continuation of No 10) received herewith. D/W.FJ	herewith (1)
		4.2.0.2.	L/Cpl. W.B.R. of "B" Coy was killed by a shell. The only ne that came near. D/W.FJ	
	29/9/15	8 a.m.	Battalion remained in trenches awaiting opening of bombardment. Artillery bombardment opened. Enemy Arty. conspicuously absent. Copy of 15th Divisional Order No 10 received, directing the charge of 15th Divisional Objective in the attack D/W.FJ	
			Steady bombardment continued. Enemy Arty. still absent. A few shells came near our position only (in the morning) although there are 3 batteries through which the trench runs. Operation Order No 7 issued by Commanding Officer. The Brigade decided to-day that all orders regarding machine guns in action should be issued through Commanding Officer only, that is in action after starting off the guns should come directly under the orders of the Commanding Officer. D/W.FJ	

Army Form C. 2118.

WAR DIARY
or
INTELLIGENCE SUMMARY.
(Erase heading not required.)

Instructions regarding War Diaries and Intelligence Summaries are contained in F.S. Regs., Part II. and the Staff Manual respectively. Title pages will be prepared in manuscript.

Place	Date	Hour	Summary of Events and Information	Remarks and references to Appendices
GRENAY– VERMELLES MAIN LINE	1/7/15	9 a.m.	Germans were searching with heavy shell for batteries in our vicinity. Brigade flew about freely. One was setting on the French recover moved to the fore.	
		3.30pm	C.O. had conference of Coy. Commanders, S.O., M.G.O., M.O., Bombing Officer to discuss the attack, particularly on LOOS so one of the objectives and details of the attack.	
			The C.O. did this according to attending a Brigade conference at 2 p.m.	
		5 p.m.	As this battalion moves into the front line trenches to-morrow at- in order to take part in the first line of an assault on the German position appended is a summary to date of movements of this battalion.	
	4/7/15		Battalion advance arose	
	2/7/15		Details left for France via SOUTHAMPTON & HAVRE	
	8/7/15		Battalion (less details) left for FRANCE via BOULOGNE–FOLKESTONE	
	9/7/15 – 15/7/15		Battalion reached billets in SAN SPETTE.	

Army Form C. 2118.

WAR DIARY
or
INTELLIGENCE SUMMARY
(Erase heading not required.)

Seaforth from 24-9-15 — 31-12-15

Place	Date	Hour	Summary of Events and Information	Remarks and references to Appendices
VERMELLES – GRENAY LINE.	24/9/15	5 pm	The Battalion started moving up into position in front line for jumping off for the attack. The going was very slow owing to the later state of the ground, and the movement of troops along the trenches. The supply of water for the night was a problem. There was about by any amount men carrying of water — also — tins of water. There supplies water, and also for filling water-bottles before leaving the trenches. The battalion was in position ready for attack about midnight.	The whole of this narrative relates to Appendices — there is no statement of anything else except Draft.
	25/9/15	3.34am	Intimation received from the Brigade that Zero Time — the time at which the discharge of Gas for forty minutes would commence — was 5.50 a.m. Zero letters for the gas was as follows	
			MINUTES. 0 — 6 cylinders of gas on offer...	
			0.12 — 0.20 smoke	
			0.20 running concurrently with Gas	
			0.32 — 0.40 6 more cylinders on after the other up first start	
			0.38 smoke again —	
			0.40 All gas offset: Smoke thickened up with triple candles Assault.	
			The morning was a dull grey morning with a light wind; but the wind did not seem	

WAR DIARY
or
INTELLIGENCE SUMMARY.
(Erase heading not required.)

Army Form C. 2118.

Place	Date	Hour	Summary of Events and Information	Remarks and references to Appendices

to be, and that no time to be particularly favourable for our own fire. Draft was at the last moment whether fire could be kept; but at 5.50 a.m. programme was proceeded with. A considerable amount of fire rolled back over our own trenches, and what with the Thunder Very Lights (according to report by a shell-lit) a good many men of the Leading Company were "gassed" and were never able to leave the trenches at all.

The German artillery very quickly took fire after the gas commenced, and first opened & shrapnel on our trenches. There were some casualties in the trenches, but at 6.30 pm the men, having then punctually got out had an issue of rum, charged the attack in splendid spirit. [Cpl. A. G. Lavehill killed in the leading platoon of "A" Coy. followed before the men got to the attack.] and the two leading platoons of "A" Coy. followed by the remaining two platoons, ought soon on the German trenches.

It seems as of Lieutenants Curtis among some of the men, whether owing to the infanticide Curtis that from took the gas, the attack was to precede. The Officer Commanding decided to alter to intentions regarding his own movements, and to convey the assurance to all that the attack was on, himself one forward on the parapet at the test of "B" Coy. instead of at the test of "C" Co clearly expected.

WAR DIARY or INTELLIGENCE SUMMARY

had not followed After Coy without loss; until — rather, indeed, only a few minutes after starting, the whole battalion was launched to the attack.

The failure to have fixed a definite delay in the event of abandonment of the gas programme, any suffering to be necessary being recessary to be regretted. Even to all, this would have avoided all uncertainty, and left the attack free from the danger of being robbed of vigour and decision, when the fortune and great necessary to it was, the gas programme was adhered to in circumstances which could never be favourable. It was a question, therefore, whether, with reference to our "gas", was in itself calculated to give confidence to the leading troops, of going them the assurance of something preceding them in the van of the assault; it, on the other hand, the doubtful success of the gas owing to the unfavourable nature of the wind must have rather this moral effect of the force; at the casualties at caused in our ranks hopes on friends and ? before against it. With regard to the enemy, any advantage of the gas must in the circumstances of the case have been far more to alarm and counteraction consequent on an element of surprise than to

WAR DIARY or INTELLIGENCE SUMMARY

Actual losses from its destructive effect. It may have caused the Germans to leave their trenches more quickly and withdrawn into loss, as the never mentioned of the enemy - infantry was probably absent from the first steps of the bombardment. This in passing the enemy's first line of trenches were commented, chiefly in numbers and in the general effects + their losses were probably for the greatest part due to artillery fire; as, the fact that the Germans were led him well cut by our preliminary bombardment of the position rather than without good reason without reason obstacles in the first line offences. Any officers, accompanying this assault to get over him wounded without seeing the Germans were, being hit near the Commanding Officer was wounded severely near the German aircraft and by by shrapnel, Capt C.G. Ross hill was killed with many of the Cy close to him about 40m, also near the German wire; Capt H.S. Munro Commanding "B" Cy, was mortally hit about the same front; Lt Roger Ryfe Renwick was killed not far from our own trenches; Lt R.C. Millar was also killed, and Lt Calder found the trenches and wounded in the front rank.

Notwithstanding the losses in officers and in NCOs and men in the

WAR DIARY or INTELLIGENCE SUMMARY

Attack had started well. The men firmed though the gaps in our own wire and formed up beyond in good order - then there drew steadily on the German line. The German resistance broke before the start of the assault; and with great rapidity progress was continued to the Second German line. Before there was reached Troops & Platoons were down, severely hit; and the remaining Coy. Commander, Capt. R.M. Powell was put out of action by a bullet wound. Several more subalterns were also wounded; and the officers remaining were few, when the attack found the Second German line and faced the German defences on LOOS itself. Machine guns in front of the village were put out of action; and then automatically all Troops withdrew from the left and put on the right flank for hand fighting in the outskirts. The remnants of the T.R. moved with into line extending to the North of the Town, and kept pushing forward. At places cover was scarce until the bombers had cleared houses from which machine guns were firing, and chipper the snipers found from the flanks. The work done by the Bombers in facilitating the advance was

WAR DIARY
or
INTELLIGENCE SUMMARY
(Erase heading not required.)

Army Form C. 2118.

Place	Date	Hour	Summary of Events and Information	Remarks and references to Appendices

most invaluable. Many prisoners were accounted for, and many were taken prisoners from the ravine, and although by the Germans, R.L. Brown helping to full. Guns had been taken to the crest of the ridge by Sgt. R. Mc Phail of "D" Coy. by the Stokenforth Kiln.

The good work by the attack had been flourished indeed; and the success attained promised to exceed the most sanguine expectations. The first line Trenches had been taken in ten to fifteen minutes & these but few and stiffly held, and the Germans who had not men with machine gun fire did not await the assault. The second line, which covered Loos itself was taken with almost equal rapidity; and the garrison withdrew into the Town, or fell back to the lines of defence further in rear. Those remaining in the Town fell after a desperate and bitter house to house fighting and were virtually all went a refuge for the enemy. Bayonets had to be used freely firing detachments carrying on individual and isolated encounters; and in the general melée, men of the different Battalions of the Brigade inevitably became mixed. There was a general drift towards

WAR DIARY or INTELLIGENCE SUMMARY

Army Form C. 2118.

of the fighting through the thin French
line - mixed - up units of the 14th Brigade were emerging from Linge, and
ascending the western slopes of the Hill, having covered a distance of over
2000 yards to the front. On the left, they met and became still further
mixed with men of the 116 Brigade, who had been attacking on the left;
and had even among them men of the 117 London Division, who were
attacking on the right.

It was difficult from such movements to follow the movements of the pts.
Sofar the, as a separate and distinct white [unit?] the 16r was broken up,
into one or two sections here in such and acting in accordance
with similar sections of other battalions. So some of these sections were
partially destroyed in efforts it is probably impossible now to gather but [recent?] the thing of
the orders given by individuals based by related bodies of the men. All
that can be done is to give an account of the causes of events in which
the [crossed out] officers, N.C.O, and men of the Battalion took part.

In proceeding beyond ROOS, a large Roadway took place in the

WAR DIARY or INTELLIGENCE SUMMARY

Battalions under these conditions attempting no doubt to begin with, the advance on a front of roughly 800 yards attempted the advance against the Gas and smoke, Red Fort familiar landmarks from rest, but now clear of our own trenches the men broke, and the fighters of LOOS formed an unfavourable guide, now that the fighters towers were famous. Those not now found themselves in an unfamiliar landscape, and were forced at once to rely on their maps for guidance. There, however, the familiarity former had at once failed him.

Moving forward according to orders, the Attack ought to have left LOOS on its right rear, and proceeded on a due Easterly direction to the CITÉ ST AUGUSTE. The factors known were then that up to gave the Attack a wrong direction, the fighters of LOOS were detected at the Westerly end of a advance that runs thousand in a south-Easterly direction. The men taken forth from follow the line of the advance, swinging therefore from LOOS through the fighters, were drawn a away in a south-Easterly direction. The front of the after of Hill 70

WAR DIARY
or
INTELLIGENCE SUMMARY.
(Erase heading not required.)

Army Form C. 2118.

Place	Date	Hour	Summary of Events and Information	Remarks and references to Appendices

itself confirmed this movement, with the result that the further advance — attack of being directed against the CITE ST AUGUSTE was deflected towards the CITE ST LAURENT and the strong German salient forming the northerly defence of LENS, subsequent fire from what made further confirm the attack in this direction. After the town of LOOS was taken there was for the moment no German resistance. In fact from 1 or 2 officers the spirit of the attack when I met that of following came over them. Very little shell-fire was being directed against the hill from enemy's batteries; and what infantry had escaped from LOOS had been driven off the hill, and had hastily made — what was left of it — but their line of defence in seemingly disorganised faced by any opposition the spirit of the attack shewed a kind of holiday mood came over the men. Myself up and disorganised by the strict fighting in LOOS, and without officers they started rather than advanced up HILL 70, and informally anti themselves out, men of the same unit cursing one another, on the crest of the hill there was uncertainty and hesitation as to what to do, and on the part of officers plenty not confirmed as to the situation location. Those "side" having advanced over the crest of Hill 70 were lying with their right upon PITS 17, and their left extending beyond the

1577 Wt. W.10791/1773 500,000 1/15 D. D. & L. A.D.S.S./Forms/C. 2118.

WAR DIARY or INTELLIGENCE SUMMARY

DYNAMYTIERE N. of the CITÉ ST LAURENT.
PITS No IV a German battery just in front of the mine buildings of Pits No IV a German battery was still firing; it was impossible for the infantry to advance on these, so a British Heavy battery was ordered the neighbouring ground apparently searching for the German guns. Shortly afterwards the German battery ceased fire, and men were seen running along the railway-embankment towards the defences around the DYNAMITIERE. While the night was thus filled up, a forward movement had begun further on the left, apparently with the intention of threatening to the next arranged objective, and — our failure to procure the advance of the attack — with the idea that the CITÉ ST LAURENT (which was not in the most generally carried) even the CITÉ ST AUGUSTE.

The Confirmation which the rapidity of the British advance had caused in the German lines was evidenced by the fact that the enemy was strongly not in position in ST LAURENT awaiting an advance, but could be seen running rapidly to and fro furiously to their strong points in honor at sunset not unlikely so if they were preparing a counter attack in which they crossed the British attack to await orderly Entrenchments and to suck to Support. LENS.

1577 Wt. W.10791/1773 500,000 1/15 D. D. & L. A.D.S.S./Forms/C. 2118.

WAR DIARY or INTELLIGENCE SUMMARY

Army Form C. 2118.

(Erase heading not required.)

Instructions regarding War Diaries and Intelligence Summaries are contained in F. S. Regs., Part II. and the Staff Manual respectively. Title pages will be prepared in manuscript.

Place	Date	Hour	Summary of Events and Information	Remarks and references to Appendices
			For the moment the fire of the enemy seemed to concert only of machine gun fire from the strongly entrenched salient at the DYNAMITIERE; but this was to prove sufficient to check all further advance of the 4th Brigade. The fire was to frequent volume to make movement on the bare slope of the hill behind; and, although the Turkish machine guns seemed from the sound of the firing to have gathered in front of the DYNAMITIERE, they were powerless to make possible any further advance of the Turkish line. Time, as it happened, worked for the Germans and against us. The Turkey flew from a second line, as it had been the to subject did not materialize; and no new forces, tho two training, and while the line expected its ammunition it failed to make progress, together for the moment had ceased between the artillery and the infantry. Only the Battery that were firing into PUITS 12 continued its fire, and from the front of the infantry who were for the moment the out encroached. If the fire of this very heavy battery could have been diverted to the DYNAMITIERE, advance into the CITÉ ST LAURENT thought not possible in the breve of the Brigade and the second night have been possible.	
		11.30 a.m.	So it was the Enemy in the CITÉ ST LAURENT were reinforced, and about half-past eleven a desperate development volume of machine-gun fire. It had come to	

1577 Wt.W10791/1773 500,000 1/15 D. D. & L. A.D.S.S./Forms/C. 2118.

WAR DIARY
or
INTELLIGENCE SUMMARY.
(Erase heading not required.)

Army Form C. 2118.

Place	Date	Hour	Summary of Events and Information	Remarks and references to Appendices

Thus that the attack of the 44th Batt'n of Fusiliers had run its last against a strong roll in

DYNAMITIERE Ridge by accident or by design the Germans had succeeded in bringing about this result. "In Dynamitieire Wester, if they are adequately manned before our troops have penetrated the LENS' defences without artillery preparation & supported by our own guns — have shown that without reinforcements and without further support from the rear, it further advance was actually impossible; indeed, in the contrary, that in view of the dispersed position of the conquered difficulties of supply of ettles of the Panzlows machine gun fire of the enemy — a retirement was necessary to the care of the Western slopes of the hill. In view of the messy-up condition of units, and the difficulties of in the circumstances of establishing a working frame-work of command, it was unlikely that this retirement would be conducted in the best order. As a matter of fact it caused in some degree to be a regular military quarter, and the men got back the best way they could, being followed up by a strong Enemy counter-attack. The situation for the moment offered extent, and it looked as if the retreating men should be rolled off the hill.

In the meantime however it appears that steps were made by some men under Lt. Col. Wallace of the 10th ... in stopping themselves in ... down the ...

WAR DIARY
or
INTELLIGENCE SUMMARY.
(Erase heading not required.)

Army Form C. 2118.

Place	Date	Hour	Summary of Events and Information	Remarks and references to Appendices
			Western edge of the hill, & advance of the also, there was a want in which men could gather; and these this position served to help officers to deal with the situation.

Lt. Johnston R.E. endeavoured to rally men and put them in the known work on the left front of the German trench. Capt. Inst. Paris, A/y Adjutant Ho gathered a string line of men on the front, and was joined there by Lt. S.K.O. Ingram 8th Leinsters, where left—though this remaining officer r we after to form a nucleus of that battalion. Machine guns were stuck into position, ammunition collected, the men steadied; and when the German counter attack appeared over the crest of the hill, it was instantly checked by the volume of fire developed. Unfortunately, however, it had proved impossible to precipitate cases of grenits to men, and tell the German help; and to the great loss of our side this along front meant again into the German hands. It was no short 1/am; and from hence forward it was becoming to held on as tenaciously as possible to the position occupied.

In the course of the afternoon the O/C 9th Lafor the received a message from Head— | |

WAR DIARY
or
INTELLIGENCE SUMMARY.
(Erase heading not required.)

Army Form C. 2118.

Place	Date	Hour	Summary of Events and Information	Remarks and references to Appendices

God-sent guards to the effect that the Brigadier had moved forward to LOOS, starting over his command to Capt Angus 10th London. The Brigade Staff HQrs reported left of Landrecies 1st Cameron Hrs been officer in the Field, and both sent for — called to Bde. Headquarters to report. They found the Brigadier in a cellar with Major Harvey, Adjt, Major, Colonel Green of the 7th K.O. Royal Scots, the Colonel and adjutant of the 9th Royal Scots, and Major Moore of the Divisional Staff, and Majr ____ as a result of the conference then held, it was decided to relieve the 44th Inf. Bde.; Colonel Green, who was taking over the 44th to sort them out of Hill 70 with the 75th Inf. Bde. who occupied the situation notified, it Battalions would be relieved in the order — Seaforths, Camerons, Black Watch, Dorset, Gordons.

On returning to the Hill, Colonel Green took over from Colonel Sandilands, who was on the rear line of defence, and one Cameron Hrs sent in to the forward trench were immediately withdrawn and that Bn. relieve first. The O.C. Gordons then appreciated his position to Colonel Green and pointed out that both flanks of the position exposed on the forward front were in the air, and the left flank seriously menaced by the German troops. Capt Roig was instructed that the was effect the evacuation of all troops from the forward trenches, to cover

WAR DIARY
or
INTELLIGENCE SUMMARY
(Erase heading not required.)

Army Form C. 2118.

Place	Date	Hour	Summary of Events and Information	Remarks and references to Appendices

Thereafter, withdrew to our battalion. There was done; and on parading R.Co. about 60 strong on the S.W. side of LOOS he retired to the Brigadier & all that remained in being of the 8th Norfolk dropped into 1 Battalion and 35 other ranks. The Medical Officer of the Bn. remained in LOOS attending wounded men who we trust were not & others constantly exposed to destruction from the intense Galle- fire to which the Germans were subjecting the place, no doubt to harry the retreating battalions that were now crossing up, enacting the shattered houses. The 8th Norfolk who made their way back to QUALITY STREET where they rested awhile, and thence they had succeeded for the night to the VERMELLES–GRENAY line, from which they had started on the afternoon of the 7th September, looking back over this brief period of 30 hours, or so in the light of the experience of this battalion two far the attack had succeeded as planned, and adapted.

(5) The spirit in which the ashes was conceived was abundantly justified by the event. "The transit to its battle, in a certain length of front got driven out of it, and must not be retaken after continuous efforts." The capital fumble "They are no retreat out continuous front system thoroughly" delay is usually the chief cause of failure and heavy casualties. Not form G.S. 164(a) L. 6.9.15

1577 Wt. W10791/1773 500,000 1/15 D. D. & L. A.D.S.S./Forms/C. 2118.

WAR DIARY
or
INTELLIGENCE SUMMARY
(Erase heading not required.)

Army Form C. 2118.

Place	Date	Hour	Summary of Events and Information	Remarks and references to Appendices

The urgency of the result of the attack thus not its nightmare inevitably the problem — when of the swift and miserable advance from objective to objective, the enemy now being allowed to recover from the initial shock on his front line trenches. Subsequently the attacking infantry (M bn) bbpbys and men cannot act independently the task work which they had been instructed. Forming the open - led of the attack, and playing they were looking in vain for other things, they await the by the 15th man orders and opened all doors. No further objectives were reached. For what reason?

(a) Because of the enemy's thinning - threateningly - defence locations of the defences of the strong thicker entrenchments covering the town of LENS. The enemy line was attempting to push forward in an easterly direction serious menace to any attack, and engaged itself frontally against the LENS defences, because the attack lost direction, and lurching its assault on the salient instead of leaving fact on its right rear, to be either neutralised CITÉ ST. AUGUSTE. As a result the attack by allowing itself to be checked by the powerful machine or dragged into an attack on the strong LENS defences gun post at the DYNAMITIÈRE, but time which allowed the enemy to bring up its reserves, and destroyed itself,

WAR DIARY or INTELLIGENCE SUMMARY

Army Form C. 2118.

(i) because, to put it otherwise, the further advance from Hill 70 was not properly officered and supported. (ii) A specific provision did not appear to be held off to dig in on the forward slope of the Hill, with the Sunken road as a Keep or strong point behind and to to form a strong defensive flank against the LENS Salient. Direct instructions to that effect were given in Operation Order No 17. — Confirmation — of 19.9.15 of H. of Bde. The Bde. Order runs "The Brigade having taken Hill 70 must hold on to the most defensible "CITÉ ST AUGUSTE." "Route is to be the "4th Brigade, the Divisional reserve, will move in accordance the necessary order for consolidating their position against hostile attack from the direction of LENS."

(ii) The supports which should have made good the Hill promptly did not come up. "The Brigade, their first reaches Hill 70 to be responsible for detailing a sufficient force to consolidate and hold it, until troops from the divisional reserve are pushed up to take it over." — 15th Div. Operation Order No 70. 21.9.15 (H) The 45th Div. Operation Order antedated the advance reserve arrival on the Hill 70 as always after dark.

(H) The result was that, so far as the success of the attack was concerned, at the End of the day the fifth objective was partially lost. So far described, the Enemy were able to bring up their reserves, to drive a shattering fire into the advance and then to drive it back to the Western slope, and recovery their own work which they had not defended in the morning, and which in a had not occupied either, not except by troops detailed to dig themselves in for the purpose. The east of Hill 70 was left weak from the front, and free there for the taking at any time, for recovery without defeats, by a successful counter attack.

WAR DIARY
or
INTELLIGENCE SUMMARY.
(Erase heading not required.)

Army Form C. 2118.

Place	Date	Hour	Summary of Events and Information	Remarks and references to Appendices
			On balance, therefore, the attack succeeded in the brilliant dash with which it captured its first few objectives. Beyond that it failed. It failed to consolidate the final position gained. Its subsequent direction of attack; and it failed to continue its advance in the direction ordered. The failure in both cases probably arose from the very nature of the attack — its great offensive outlawry. The same was fairly to be expected, and partly perhaps it was. A considerable number of men were either dead or alive fell into the enemy's hands on the far side of Hill 70; but if the attack had not been checked at the CÔTE ST LAURENT and had gone on as originally intended to the CÔTE ST AUGUSTE, (unsupported by a forced battery (g b) finally crest of Hill 70 while not a man would have returned. On the failure to secure the afterwards other part of the there was yet time, and the enemy had not recovered himself and worked up the return of his fire, but at this time even when the heights were practically empty to enforce the attack to the crest falling back into the enemy's lands and at most upon the forward slopes of them. Indeed had only the Branch programme attack fell forward slope of the hill for this have, and sufficient might have been so-fiercely to come up in that time; at the same time if the hill had been properly secured, it might have been permanently retained — any further advance being made on so dis it was in consequence attempts not dray had themselves on the near German trenches on Hill 70; and no further further advance found towards "the furthest furthest points."	

1577. Wt. W10791/1773 500,000 1/15 D. D. & L. A.D.S.S./Forms/C. 2118.

WAR DIARY or INTELLIGENCE SUMMARY

Army Form C. 2118.

Place	Date	Hour	Summary of Events and Information	Remarks and references to Appendices
VERMELLES– GRENAY LINE	26/9/15		The Bombers have broken down at one of its most pressing points during the night before the 25th September. The remainder of the Battalion who would relieve them were engaged in carrying ammunition into LOOS, along the LENS road. 2/Lt Duncan was hit. On the Sunday morning, just after the small party had been sent up to relieve, a message was received ordering them to proceed to join the Old British Line immediately. O.C. the LENS road by 9.30 a.m. The message arrived about 10.30 a.m. but after the men that had been transported were so ordered. Capt. C.C. Droysh, 2 Majors and 2/Lt. Hudson and Capt. Doyle Smyth were Scout Officer proceeded to Brigade Headquarters at QUALITY STREET to report. It was reported beyond the Battalion who was not now carry out the received instructions that the 9th Battalion who were now in MELLES– GRENAY line. Major Boyce of the 18th Batt. Staff was not, and he warned the Battalion to hold itself in readiness to receive instructions to proceed to the British line. The orders to do this was received in the early afternoon, and the Battalion moved its position immediately afterward. About 4 p.m. in the afternoon orders were received to move on to the old GERMAN line, taking care of gas. The 7/–, and Regiment recaptured the German ...	

1577 Wt. W10791/1773 500,000 1/15 D. D. & L. A.D.S.S./Forms/C. 2118.

Army Form C. 2118.

WAR DIARY
or
INTELLIGENCE SUMMARY.
(Erase heading not required.)

Instructions regarding War Diaries and Intelligence Summaries are contained in F. S. Regs., Part II. and the Staff Manual respectively. Title pages will be prepared in manuscript.

Place	Date	Hour	Summary of Events and Information	Remarks and references to Appendices
MALINGARBE	26/9/15		The trench, as found it full of gas, the Germans were at this time despatching still. Fire over the still area as they had been doing during the whole day. The Staffords this with the rest of the Brigade frequently moved over, and re-captured the old German Support line. They remained here until near midnight, when orders were received to send a killing party to MAZINGARBE to meet the Regt. Captain. He. Ev. subsequently moved off, and went into billets in MAZINGARBE. There were no casualties during this stay, and the day had been without incident, save for the reappearance of considerable numbers of Infield troops to a diminished extent from the direction of HILL 70.	
	28/9/15	9.30 a.m.	Bn. remained in MAZINGARBE, re-organising, re-equipping, and checking rolls, and endeavouring to trace return of casualties to Officers, N.C.O. and men. Several men rejoined the Bn. who had been with other units; grades, and details the was recovered; and baggage and stores collected. — Routine Orders Published. ※ RED ROAD, — NŒUX-LES-MINES — K.18.a	※ Ref. Appx 000 hrs sheet 36 C.
			Bn. marched off to HOUCHIN via HOUCHIN. First line transport accompanied unit.	
			On arrival at HOUCHIN Command of the Bn. was taken over by Capt. John E. Kendall Lafitte Wo., late Adjutant 23rd London Regiment, who joined for duty. Temp allotted for	

1577 Wt.W10791/1773 500,000 1/15 D. D. & L.   A.D.S.S./Forms/C. 2118.

WAR DIARY
INTELLIGENCE SUMMARY

Place	Date	Hour	Summary of Events and Information	Remarks and references to Appendices
HOUCHIN			Command at HOUCHIN as in Column B.	
			"A" Coy — Capt. S. Murray	
			"B" Coy — Lt. F. Holmes	
			"C" Coy — Capt. G.R.O. Hodgson	
			"D" Coy — Lt. E.K.O. Ferguson	
	28/9/15		Capts. S. Murray, G.R. Anderson, C.C. Smyth, Lt. E.K.O. Ferguson were charged to B.	
			Lt. E.W. Duncan was detailed to make an inventory of the kits of officers who were casualties, and to despatch the same in due form.	
	30/9/15		On the 27th inst. the C.O.F. Commander had decided that it was impossible to send out parties to bury our dead on the field of battle of the 25th. To-day Lt. J. Holmes and 10 men were proceeded to QUALITY STREET for the work of burial.	
			Mr. Renaud at HOUCHIN. Recommendations for honors and rewards were this day forwarded to our Bgd. Adm.	
	1/10/15	a.m.	151, along with the no. of 7th "Toes and 9th Lorraine (Princes) was inspected and —	
			Obtained by General Sir Henry Rawlinson Sir Henry Rawlinson conveyed the thanks of the Army and of the British, to the Royal Naval & Crown, Brigadier-General Grant Wilkinson, and its officers and men of the Div. as a Stipple. For the work they had done during the great battle, the officially mentioned the change of the Suffolk Div. and of Black Watch. Regretting that it had not further trouble to give to the attack to effect it was intended to Sohencourt the Lys Flat in the futures these Battalions would see complete victory crown their efforts.	

WAR DIARY or INTELLIGENCE SUMMARY

Army Form C. 2118.

(28)

Place	Date	Hour	Summary of Events and Information	Remarks and references to Appendices
	15/7/15		Battalion went into billets for the night at **HAZEBROUCK**	
	16/7/15		Battalion went into billets for the night at BUSNETTES.	
	17/7/15 – 1/8/15		Battalion was in billets at HOUCHIN	
	2/8/15 – 5/8/15		Battalion was in billets in SOUTH MAROC in brigade reserve Sub-Sector W.1.	
	6/8/15 – 10/8/15		Battalion in trenches, Subsector W.1.	
	11/8/15 – 16/8/15		Battalion in billets at MAZINGARBE. – Divisional Reserve	
	17/8/15		Battalion proceeded to LE PHILOSOPHE and went into billets for the night	
	18/8/15 – 26/8/15		Battalion in Trenches Sub-sector X1	
	27/8/15 – 30/8/15		Battalion in billets in LE PHILOSOPHE in Brigade Reserve	
	31/8/15 – 7/9/15		Battalion in Divisional Reserve at NOEUX-LES-MINES	
	7/9/15		Battalion in close billets and bivouac at MAZINGARBE	
	8/9/15 – 19/9/15		Battalion in Brigade Reserve at NOEUX-LES-MINES	
	19/9/15 – 23/9/15		Battalion in GRENAY-VERMELLES MAIN LINE Trenches	

BATTALION OPERATION ORDER NO. 1.

OPERATION ORDER No. 1. BY LIEUT. COL. N.A. THOMSON.
COMMANDING 8TH SEAFORTH HIGHLANDERS. 22-9-15.

		Signature for Receipt.
No. 1.	C.O's. Copy.	
2.	"A" Company.	*[signed]* 6.10 p.m.
3.	"B" "	*[signed]*
4.	"C" "	*[signed]*
5.	"D" "	*[signed]* 6 p.m.
6.	Signalling Officer.	*[signed]*
7.	Machine Gun Officer.	*[signed]* 6.30 p.m.
8.	Medical Officer.	*[signed]* S. Robinson
9.	Transport Officer & Quartermaster.	*[signed]* 7.30 p.m.
10.	War Diary.	

SECRET

Copy No 10

OPERATION ORDER No. 1. BY LIEUT. COL. N.A.THOMSON, COMMANDING 8TH BATT. SEAFORTH HIGHLANDERS.

22/9/15

1. The 8th Seaforth Highlanders will form part of the assaulting line of the 44th Infantry Brigade in an attack on the German position, in which the 15th Division will take a principal part.

2. The attack is being preceded by a heavy artillery bombardment, day and night, for four days, up to the moment of the Infantry assault on the fifth day.

3. During the preliminary stages of the artillery bombardment the 8th Seaforth Highlanders will remain in the GRENAY-VERMELLES line. On 24th September, the night before the assault, they will occupy trenches X.1. between Boyau 7.b. (inclusive) and Boyau 8.c. (exclusive).
They will move up to the trenches as follows :-
"A" Company, followed by "A" Coy. Black Watch, will leave the GRENAY-VERMELLES trenches at 5.0 p.m., proceed by Southern Up and T.21 to relieve the 10th Gordons as under :-
    "A" Company. Seaforth Highlanders. via T.8.
    "A"   "   Black Watch.   via T.7.
"K" Coy. and "B" Coy. will arrange to leave SOUTHERN UP clear for passing of "A" Coy. Black Watch.
"K" Company will occupy side trench beyond railway embankment. "B" Coy. will close in on "C" Coy.
The Gordons relieved by "A" Coy. Seaforth Highlanders, leave by 8.b. 26.a. 8. part of 7, and 6.
Gordons relieved by "A" Coy. Black Watch leave by 6.

"A" Coy. Seaforth Highlanders, will leave a guide at a point where trench 21 cuts trench 6, to report to "B" Coy. Seaforth Highlanders, when the Gordons relieved by the Black Watch, are clear of that point on their way out.
At 5.30 p.m. the Seaforth Highlanders, in order "B", "C" and "D" Coys. followed by Black Watch in order "B", "C", and "D" Coys. will proceed by Southern Up and Trench 21, where, on receipt of report from the Seaforth guide, they will file into their allotted places, Seaforth Highlanders via trench 21 and 8.
The allotted places of the Seaforth Highlanders are as under :-
    "A" Company.   Firing Line.   7.B. - 8.C.
    "B"   "   Support.   7.B. - 8.C.
    "C"   "   Trench 26.A. and part of 8.
    "K" & "D"   "   Trench 21, between 8 and 23.
The Machine Guns will move up in rear of the battalion to Machine Gun positions.

4. In making the assault the 8th Seaforth Highlanders will be formed up in depth on a front of two platoons.
The Black Watch will attack on our Right on a front of two platoons.
The 10th Scottish Rifles, as part of the 46th Infantry Brigade, will attack simultaneously on our Left.
Following the 8th Seaforth Highlanders and Black Watch will be :-
    2 Sections. Royal Engineers.
    2 Platoons, 9th Gordon Highlanders (Pioneers).
    7th Cameron Highlanders on a front of 4 platoons.
    10th Gordon Highlanders in Reserve.

5. The 8th Seaforth Highlanders will attack on the following objectives :-

    1st. German front and Support Trenches.
    2nd. German second line trenches.
    3rd. LOOS Village.
    4th. PUITS No. 15.
    5th. German work in H.31.d.
    6th. CITE St. AUGUSTE.
    7th. Highground North of LOISON-SOUS-LENS.

The Right of the 8th Seaforth Highlanders will advance on a mean Compass bearing of 118 deg. magnetic (variation 13 deg.) from G.28.C.5.4½. to H.31.C.10.7.

Our Left will advance on a mean Compass bearing of 113 deg. from G.28.C.6½.9., through houses at G.29.D.4.4. to houses at G.30.C.5.3., thereafter on a bearing of 128 deg. magnetic to H.31.A.10.1.

6. In delivering the assault the 8th Seaforth Highlanders will push on without delaying. Having broken the enemy's front system of trenches (their first objective) they will not stay to occupy or consolidate the positions won, nor to dig communications back to our present trenches. They will drive home the attack to the full power of the battalion, and will press on from objective to objective, until the final objective is reached.

7. The assault will be delivered by the Seaforth Highlanders (on a front of two platoons) in the order "A", "B", "C", and "D" Coys. Each Company will ensure the flow is properly maintained by at once moving into the place of the one in front directly the latter moves on.

8. Bombing squads will move on the outer flank of their platoons.

9. Machine Gun Sections will advance in the attack as follows :-
    One Machine Gun with the two rear platoons of "B" Coy.
    Two   "   "   "   "   "   "   "C" "
    One   "   "   "   "   "   "   "D" "

The Machine Gun Officer will make arrangements for moving off his guns in that order. During the action he will be responsible for the tactical handling of his guns, subject to the orders of the Commanding Officer.

10. The following Officers will not accompany the battalion in the attack :-
        Capt. G. Murray.
        " C.C. Forsyth.
        " G.R. Anderson.

These Officers, according to special instructions already issued, will report to 1st. Line Transport at NOEUX-LES-MINES, at 5 p.m., on the 24th September.

Lieut. F. Holmes, as already detailed, will be in charge of Brigade Machine Gun Limbers with reserve ammunition at MAZINGARBE CHATEAU.

Lieut. G.W. Duncan will remain with the 1st. Line Transport at NOEUX-LES-MINES.

11. The actual hour of the assault will be issued later. There will be a special gas preparation lasting exactly 40 minutes immediately prior to the assault.

O.C. "A" Coy. will detail 18 men, under an Officer, to be (2 men per Bay) in Bays 88, 91, 94, 97, 100, 104, 107, 109, 112, (9 Bays) of Trenches X.1. at 6.45 p.m. on the 24th inst. for the purpose of operating candles during the gas discharges.

These men will precede "A" Coy. to the trenches, leaving at 4.50 p.m.

The Officer will report to the O.C. 187th (Special) Coy. R.E.

They will stand on the firing platform while the relief is carried out.

At 7 p.m. they will stand to their Bays fully equipped.

These men will come under the orders of the Commanding Officer immediately on the completion of the gas discharges.

The Officer in charge of the party will call at Battalion Headquarters at 7.p.m. to-day for further instructions.

12. To enable the men to get out of the trenches, sandbag steps are being prepared, scaling ladders placed in position, and pickets fixed in the parapet; and these will be used.

Four diagonal strips are being cut by the 10th Gordon Highlanders in our own wire for each platoon; sections will pass through these and extend beyond the wire.

13. Equipment will be in accordance with instructions issued to Coys. recently. In addition "D" Coy. will carry 25 Picks and 50 Shovels, which will be carried slung across the back with rope slings.

All ranks will have water bottles full at the moment of going over the parapet, and will wear smoke helmets rolled up ready for immediate use.

14. Each man will leave the trenches, at the actual moment of assault, carrying 220 rounds of ammunition. All ammunition used in firing from the trenches will be taken from boxes of ammunition placed in each Bay for this purpose.

An Advanced Ammunition Depot, containing 100,000 rounds of ammunition, has been made at junction of trenches 8 and 26, and will be under Battalion Sergeant Major Forbes.

There will be a Brigade Reserve Ammunition Store at QUALITY STREET, in charge of Captain Cunningham, 7th Camerons.

15. 500 Grenades, packed in boxes, (which can be carried by one man) will be stored in two forward Trench Depots.

16. Vermoral Sprayers are to be distributed along the whole of the front line trenches at equal intervals. Parties, to be detailed later, will carry forward sprayers which will be used to clear gas from enemy's trenches and dug-outs. A spare tin of solution will be taken forward with each sprayer.

17. As far as possible, the men will move over the open and will avoid going into the enemy's trenches.

Dug-outs and cellars will not be entered without smoke helmet being lowered.

18. On the night of September 24th. the Medical Officer will move with the battalion into a forward aid post, constructed where trench 21 cuts the new evacuation trench. Post is on South side of new trench and just West of 21.

19. The Signalling Officer will arrange for communication according to special instructions issued to him.

20. First Line Transport will be arranged according to special instructions issued to the Transport Officer.

21. In the event of the iron rations having to be used, only one tin in four will be opened at a time, providing four meals. All waste must be scrupulously avoided.

22. The Provost Sergeant with 5 police will report to Capt. Pearson, 10th Gordon Highlanders, at MAZINGARBE, at 4.30 p.m. on September 24th. and will remain there for the night.
Instructions regarding prisoners will be issued later.

23. Any guns captured from the enemy, which are in danger of being lost again, will be rendered useless by damaging the sights and breech mechanism.
Captured Machine Guns will be collected or broken.

24. All papers and orders will be destroyed before the advance. No papers will be carried by Officers or men except the new 1/10,000 Trench Map shewing the German Trenches only, and the 1/40,000 map, Sheet 36. C. N.W.
<u>All messages and reports will refer to one or the other of these Maps.</u>

Duncan W.P. Strang Captain.
Adj. 8th Battn. Seaforth Highlanders.

```
Copy No.  1.    C.O's. Copy.
  "       2.    "A" Company.
  "       3.    "B"   "
  "       4.    "C"   "
  "       5.    "D"   "
  "       6.    Signalling Officer.
  "       7.    Machine Gun Officer.
  "       8.    Medical Officer.
  "       9.    Transport Officer & QrMr.
  "      10.    War Diary.
```

Index..................

SUBJECT.

8th Seaforths

No.	Contents.	Date.
	October 1915.	

WAR DIARY or INTELLIGENCE SUMMARY

Army Form C. 2118.

Place	Date	Hour	Summary of Events and Information	Remarks and references to Appendices
HOUCHIN	1/10/15	a.m.	A draft of 4 N.C.O's and 64 men joined the Bn. This day, and were taken to Coys. Appointments to the Estry rank of Sgt., Cpl., and L/Cpl. were made into "A" Coy. to carry on work. — D.W.H.	
"	2/10/15	a.m.	The Bn. was inspected and addressed by Major-General MacCracken. The Hatter the officers and men for the great service they had done to themselves, to the Division, and to left-hand in the great battle of the 25th of Sep. He expressed the hope that all ranks would go on to rebuild the Bn., and reconstruct it so worthy of its reputation, making desserts to the Bn., with music of all their work. A draft was this day took as - constituting the Framed Formed of the Bn. 2 Cpls. and 2 Sgts. being sent to WISQUES for a machine-gun course. Further Appointments were this day made to N.C.O. ranks of A, C, D Coys. A charge was now made in the internal administration of the Bn. Prior to the 25th September all Specialists etc. formed a separate Coy. for purpose of drawing iti., was not sent for pay and clothing. This Coy. was now abolished, and Specialists allotted in their entire formed for all purposes to Coys. eg—Scouts — Transport to "A" Coy., Stretcher bearers to "B" Coy., Signallers to "C" Coy. and Machine-gunners to "D" Coy. The intention is to facilitate rationing, clothing, paying, and discipline of men concerned. — D.W.H.	
3/10/15			Bn. remained in HOUCHIN. It must be noted that all this period has been marked by an uncertainty as to the future movements of the Bn., doubtless these would be to the future years, in to Relieve Italians.	

Wt. W10791/1773 500,000 1/15 D.P.&L A.D.S.S./Forms/C.2118

WAR DIARY
or
INTELLIGENCE SUMMARY.
(Erase heading not required.)

Army Form C. 2118.

Place	Date	Hour	Summary of Events and Information	Remarks and references to Appendices
HEUCHIN — LILLERS	2/9/15	12 noon	The Bn. marched out of HUCHIN and proceeded to LILLERS via LES D'ROUVIN — LES MARAIS — LAGUSSIERE — MARLES LES MINES — HAUTRIEUX — LILLERS. Staff of 5 N.C.Os and 47 men fallen on the march and fallen to report sick.	Ref. Map LENS 1/2, and HAZEBROUCK 5a Sheet
	5/10/15		Training commenced — Bn. route march — Coy and specialist training, including drill and Coy of bombers. Further appointments of N.C.Os made viz. A, B, C, and D Coys. The casualties suffered among N.C.Os of the Bn. made these appointments necessary. The principle adopted is to endeavour to effect the most efficient team, and in pursuit of this principle undue regard cannot be paid to the fact that men have been & have over steps in promotion. Presumably good previous experience would be better N.C.Os for the Bn. in the circumstances than mere preference, coming out with rank from home. At any rate seriously the N.C.Os must go forward in the re-constitution of the Battalion, specially in effecting the supreme test that is that of transforming a succession of drafts into a Battalion, conscious of itself, and possessing adorned spirit in every and as spoken in the 2 Reports No 1 before its decimation in the 25th of September. Officers arrived the day and are listed to Coys as follows:— "A" Coy:— Lt. P.H.F. Swinton, Lt. T. Buchanan, Lt. G. Preston, Lt's J.K. Taylor "B" Coy:— Lt. G. Hunt, Lt. W. Murray, Lt. J.G. Duncan, Lt. T.H. Rao, Lt. J.R. Smith "C" Coy:— Lt. J. Hodgson, Lt. J.H. Harper, Lt. M. Brau, Lt. J. Howell "D" Coy:— Lt. J. Blackwood, Lt. M. Cameron, Lt. S. Cotter, Lt. D.M. Darling	

WAR DIARY
INTELLIGENCE SUMMARY

Place	Date	Hour	Summary of Events and Information	Remarks and references to Appendices
LILLERS	5/10/15		A beginning was this day made for Officers & men proceeding on leave to Gt. Britain. 2 Lieut & 3 N.C.O.s and men. "K + 9" proceeded T.D. took over duties of Asphalt Draft. Training carried on in Route march. The Bn. are beginning to approach to say nothing of exceeding the platoons than they did, the Bn. now beginning to approach to say nothing of exceeding the strength in Future Orders for the day. The following casualties officers were published in Routine Orders of the day. Killed in Action 25th Sept. — wounded 25th Sept. Admitted to Hospital. Major A.J.M. Zaneira — Capt R.A. Parnell — Capt P.C. Miller — Lieut P.V. Bayford — 2/Lt B.M. Tedder — Capt R.R. Powell — Lieut H.T. Macaulay. 2/Lt C. Le Maren 27th Sept. Major N. Fortune " Lt. J.M. Duff " 2/Lt A.W. Sunhill " 2/Lt Jas L. Hatton 27 Sept. Capt H.T. Hamer 27 Sept.	
"	6/10/15		The following casualties affecting N.C.O.s and men were published. Killed in Action - Died of Wounds - wounded and invalided to England. 11 N.C.O. & 32 men 2 N.C.O.s and 4 men 27 N.C.O.s and 49 men. Training carried on - on Route march Skeleton training, including training of Stretcher bearers, who did not possibly work under the M.O. in the 1st of Sept. Act offr supply. Lacking of Byden Reserve Lestons 507 Came carried on under (Lieutenants) Capt C.C. Smyth and D.D. & L. other ranks proceeded this day to England — R.Q.S. Next Batch of "D.Cy."	

1577 Wt. W10791/1773 500,000 1/15 A.D.S.S./Forms/C. 2118.

WAR DIARY
or
INTELLIGENCE SUMMARY.
(Erase heading not required.)

Army Form C. 2118.

Place	Date	Hour	Summary of Events and Information	Remarks and references to Appendices
LILLERS	7/9/15		The following casualties were included — that of this battalion were included — that of this Co. — 1 N.C.O and 2 men wounded.	
"	8/9/15		This day 2nd Lt. N. J. Taylor and 2 N.C.O.'s were sent on a Bombing course to Hinges. Capt. & 2/Lt Side at ALLOUAGNE. 2/Lt. C. MacMullen joined the Bn. for duty. Training carried on according to programme. Special attention being paid to care and use of arms and march discipline. An Orderly Officer was this day appointed for the Bn. 2/Lt. I. J. Howell was this day appointed Bn. Spalding Officer. The following casualties were included. Affecting N.C.O. and men of the Bn... Killed in action 25th + 26th Sept. Bros. J. Wounded. 7 N.C.O.'s 25 men. 1 N.C.O. 1 man.	
"	9/10/15		Training under Capt. And specialist arrangements. — 2/Lt. — Hac Mullen posted to "A" Coy. The following casualties included — one of wounds 1 man... Buna Larrea. — orders received for move at short notice rather unexpectedly in the forenoon.	
"	10/10/15		— orders received from 44th Inf. Bde. —	
"	12/11/15		orders received for move of the Bn. by rail to NOEUX-LES-MINES.	
"	13/11/15	5.8 pm	Bn. left LILLERS by train to fureet into billets — NOEUX-LES-MINES	
		5.30 pm	Transport, Brigade, left LILLERS and proceeded to NOEUX-LES-MINES via ALLOUAGNE — LOZINGHEN — MARLES-LES-MINES and rond just S. HOUCHIN. Capt. Mcf. Brit. Railway reported the Battalion this day for duty. D.O.&S.	

WAR DIARY
or
INTELLIGENCE SUMMARY.
(Erase heading not required.)

Army Form C. 2118.

Place	Date	Hour	Summary of Events and Information	Remarks and references to Appendices
NŒUX-LES-MINES	13/10/15	—	Arrival at NŒUX-LES-MINES ends the first forced move forward in the re-construction of the battalion. Nearly three weeks have passed since the decimation of the old battalion at LOOS. By the 26th September the battalion had moved from the line to re-constitute and refit. To-day it is moving once more towards the enemy. It remains to re-ceive from the 4th R. Bde. that units will be ready to move at the shortest notice. Extra, will be prepared to issue extra ammunition, and the unexpended portion of the day's ration will be ready for immediate issue. That has marked the interesting period. To 1st official completion of Casualties of 9/10th and 14th Battalions; 2nd drafts of officers and men fitted together as a distinct battalion; 3rd training drafts of officers and men to think and act together as a distinct battalion. The last men-tioned has to be done so as to shorten a time, that the prospect two ahead of the firing and disciplining of this battalion as a battalion having to to done in the trenches. A junior division memo for the moment to be attached in front in which the Bn has recovered in some degree from its past displacement, and is settling down to the ordinary routine of a unit of effective strength and at disposal for ordinary trench warfare. D.W.P.J.	
"	14/10/15	—	Training carried on as usual. Chining casualties published:— Died of Wounds. 1st Lieut. D.W.P.J. 1 man Killed in action 93rd dept. 3 men	

WAR DIARY

PLACE	DATE	TIME	SUMMARY OF EVENTS AND INFORMATION	REMARKS APPENDICES
NOEUX-LES-MINES	15/10/15	—	Training under Coy. and Squadt. Arrangements:— Following Casualties Published:— Killed in Action. Wded. of Wounds 9 men. 1 N.C.O. Wounded and Invalided to England. 9 N.Co's and 20 men.	
	16/10/15		Following Staff arrived and were posted to Coys. 14 N.C.Os & 195 men. 3 N.C.Os and 20 men reported for duty from the base. Training under Coy. and Squadt. Arrangements:—	D.S.P. D.S.P.
"	17/10/15		Arme Lerna. Inspection by C.O. of A & B Coys. Leave of Absence granted to 2Lt. O. of Spenton and 4 other ranks to proceed to England. 19th to 28th Oct. Following Casualties Published:— Wounded and Invalided to England. 2Lt. R.S. Payne, 1 N.C.O.M. Wounded 6 men. Awarded by Commander-in-Chief to 5/2793 Pte. David Allegan "B" Coy (since deceased) D.S.P.	D.S.P.
"	18/10/15		Training according to programme:— Following Casualties Published. Killed in Action 1 N.C.O. and 2 men.	D.S.P.
"	19/10/15		Training under Coy. Arrangements. Number of appointments to N.C.O. rank made in M.G. Section	D.S.P.
"	20/10/15		Training as usual. Following Casualties Published. Killed in Action Left 75 Wounded and Invalided to England. 2 men. 1 N.C.O. and 8 men	D.S.P.
"	21/10/15		Training as usual. Following Casualties Published. Killed in Action Left 25. 3 men. Leave of Absence granted to Capt. G. Murray, Capt. R. Robertson, from 27nd to 29 ult.	D.S.P.

WAR DIARY

PLACE	DATE	TIME	SUMMARY OF EVENTS AND INFORMATION	REMARKS APPENDICES
NOEUX-LES-MINES	22/10/15		Batt. bathed in Divisional baths. Following casualties published — Wounded and remained at duty — Off. N. Heath and 4 men.	
"	23/10/15		Training as usual. Following casualties published — 1 man. Wounded in action and on ____ [illeg.] relieved to England & evacuated immediately N. of the VERMELLES HULLUCH Rd to be taken over by us.	
"	24/10/15		Divine Service.	
"	25/10/15		Divisional Baths. Following Casualties Published. Killed in action 25th — 1 man. Left 1 man. Groups moved for move into trenches N. VERMELLES - HULLUCH road.	
"	26/10/15	9.45 am	Bat. commenced moving off from NOEUX-LES-MINES for the purpose of proceeding to the British trenches N. of the VERMELLES - HULLUCH ROAD where it relieved the 11th U.K.J. Bde. in local reserve. The 8th Battn. Kts. occupied the old German front and old British front trenches behind the new British front line occupied by the 9th Lancer Bde. from G. 12. D central HULLUCH ROAD (Spelwan) to G. 12. a. 5. 4. The relief was completed without incident in what seemed fairly promising weather. On getting into the trenches Coys devoted themselves to settling down in their portion of trenches and endeavouring to find any accommodation for the men. Coys were disposed as follows:- D Coy. 9th German front line immediately N. of HULLUCH ROAD. "B" Coy. on its Left. "C" Coy. in Old British line Trenches 2 and 3. "B" Coy in O.B.3. Bn. Headquarters were in a dug-out near the left of "D" Coy. between old German front and support lines.	

WAR DIARY

PLACE	DATE	TIME	SUMMARY OF EVENTS AND INFORMATION	REMARKS APPENDICES
TRENCHES C.T.	16/9/15		The marked feature of the line into which the Bn. has not moved is the great length of communication trenches to be kept up, this is rendered necessary owing to the fact that the trenches lie for the most part on the far country sloping to right up against the CITÉ ST ELIE and are undetected by any village in our hands. The trenches might as well be in dead ground to the enemy, because only the front lines themselves — fire and support trench — are cut on the forward side of a slope which falls gradually from the buried foot slip of VERMELLES, and only falls away again in front of the CITÉ ST ELIE: but the fact that FOSSE 8 behind the HOHENZOLLERN REDOUBT is held by the Germans exposes the whole area to observation and denies to us the VERMELLES — HULLUCH road for military use 'except at night'. Supplies are brought up after dark from the transport lines at PHILOSOPHE along this road, and dumped short of the crossing of the LOOS — HAISNES road. In taking over these trenches it is obvious at single glance that a great deal remains to be done to connect them and generally to turn them into an organic, well-jointed defensive system, then enough adequate and satisfactory (i.e. strong and dry) accommodation for trench stores and to ensure them from the front of this front of defences (the existent one situation) the most urgent necessity of the moment is further an improvement of communication trenches from front to rear, traffic between the eastern trenches and the German front line is, apart for the moment to one artery = CHAPEL ALLEY,	

WAR DIARY

PLACE	DATE	TIME	SUMMARY OF EVENTS AND INFORMATION	REMARKS APPENDICES
C.T.	26/4/15		Communication from the old German line to new British line was confirmed also to CHAPEL ALLEY - Relief, ration parties and preparation of new trench to run along this trench. DEVON LANE extending from the old British line to the old British line was to follow. The new trench and the situation was viewed from several that the maximum of work would be in the bullet interests of all concerned.	Shot
C.T.	27/4/15		Day spent in improving trenches and acquiring familiarity with trench arrangements. The turnover of trenches is extremely uncomfortable but of [unclear] work in this sector. Wade is brought to HULUCH ROAD Dump at night for this Battalions. This has to be carried by party of 200 for [unclear] to have water line, where I have in [unclear] left for use of our Battalion, and [unclear] for use [unclear] German [unclear]. As we have two Coys in old British lines supplies of water for them a problem. Orders issued for securing Soho Tanks. Today the weather and the trenches became increasingly uncomfortable the oil being frozen fell in [unclear] they have to dry-out and build [unclear] in a [unclear] to self return the [unclear] for "they - bayed". C.T.S. - having more work to do alone. — [unclear] own dugout and released [unclear] transfer charged - [unclear]. Leave of absence granted to Capt E.R. Aulran 27 Oct to 2nd Nov.	

WAR DIARY

PLACE	DATE	TIME	SUMMARY OF EVENTS AND INFORMATION	REMARKS APPENDICES
C 2	28/10/15.		Routine of cleaning, digging etc. carried out. Bomb and ammunition stores to be constructed. Orders ~~for~~ received for relieving 7th Camerons in front line on 29th. DWT	
C 2	29/10/15.	a.m. p.m.	Relief of 7th Cameron Machine Guns effected Relief of Coys. of 7th Camerons effected, relief proceeding by CHAPEL ALLEY and STONE LANE. Coys. were disposed as shown in following sketch:—	

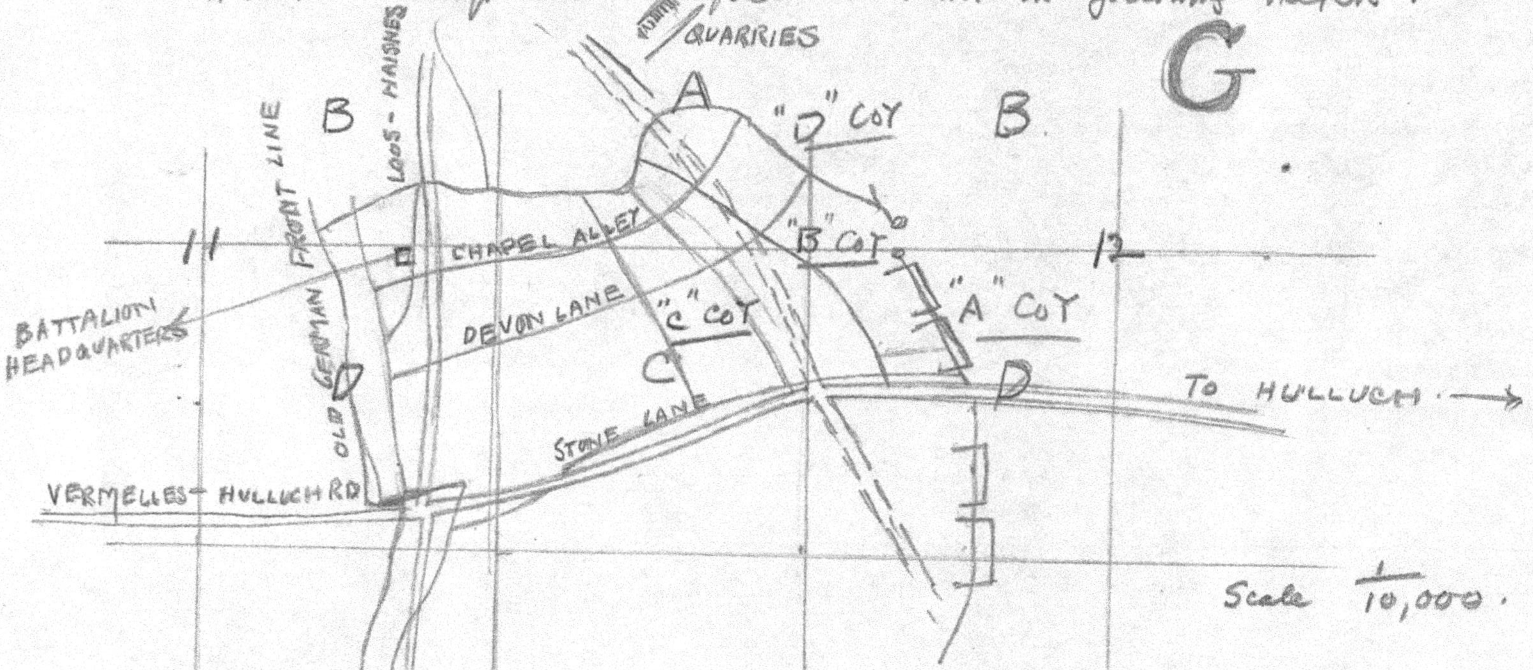

QUARRIES
A
"D" COY
B
G
B
LOOS - HAISNES
FRONT LINE
11
12
CHAPEL ALLEY
"B" COY
"A" COY
BATTALION HEADQUARTERS
DEVON LANE
"C" COY
C
OLD GERMAN
D
D
TO HULLUCH
STONE LANE
VERMELLES - HULLUCH RD
Scale 1/10,000.

WAR DIARY

PLACE	DATE	TIME	SUMMARY OF EVENTS AND INFORMATION	REMARKS APPENDICES

The front trenches are set by any means good. They are the track immediately N. of the HERLUCH SOMMER ROAD all to seen to the German line and are strict though the German lines into. This makes the rifles to places the trenches to the gun – pits being nothing than exceedingly rocky, the soft no paper parapet or trenches. For trench they captured carrying to be considered a particularly favourable or dangerous it cannot the falling of fire trenches. Other features too, made the inference the loss hyaping. As to the officers and the talk of the now of "A" Coy had never been in a fire-trench, before and regarding the renewal of filling trenches had only their training & also with no experience to guide them. They had no experience either of the danger of the real danger of trench warfare and were exposed to hazards its ordinary incidents. Especially at night such as German flares and lights into Coverwise. Perils – the illuminating character of the trenches them-selves too, was made worse by the somewhat defensive nature of the immediate surroundings of the trench line. The ground in front was little depth, topography between the Highland troops; and our own lay to our left and in front and trenches literally see by the their fire trench. It would be more to seeing of their own comrades, dead bodies to fret trips to see bodies of the fire trench was an unwelcome thing, of the enemy rather than the continually A gap in the

WAR DIARY

PLACE	DATE	TIME	SUMMARY OF EVENTS AND INFORMATION	REMARKS APPENDICES
C2	29/10/15		Relieving the right Coy. and entering it to our communication trench — STONE LANE — from front to rear. 2 of the Coy. the Servian trenches ran into close proximity with our trenches, both trying to stop Maps Heads, thus exceedingly trying the night harassment incident; out there, exceedingly trying to trenches; being warned it was set up trench as they thought. how that already begun to settle down in the morning. D/W/F	
C2	30/10/15		Day of not settling down to trench routine; and attempting to improve the trenches in some degree. 2/Lt. Mackenzie M.G. Officer was killed this day before dawn unfortunately 2/Lt. through the head, while standing at the parapet working a Machine bullet Gun Emplacement on the left of the line. D/W/F	
C2	31/10/15		Routine Duties and Work:— Party of "A" Coy reconnoitring to try some new hat an unfortunate experience, then attack to return in vicinity of their lines and a Staff rifle grenade from the Servian line came over and burst amongst them 2o S/3452 Pte J. Brown, and wound Pte J.A.S. Jameson and two others. Leave of absence granted to 2/Lt Erw Duncan aut 2N.C.O's from 2r Oct. to 6 Nov. 2/Lt H.C. Duncan appointed transport Officer in the absence of 2/Lt S.W. Duncan. 2N.C.O's and men following casualties from 16th to 26th Sept. Transferred:— Wounded and invalided to England — 2N.C.O's and 9 men D/W/F 	

Index................................

M G 5-W
14 sheets

SUBJECT.

8th Seaforths

No.	Contents.	Date.
	November 1915	

WAR DIARY

PLACE	DATE	TIME	SUMMARY OF EVENTS AND INFORMATION	REMARKS APPENDICES
Sector C.3.	1/11/15	a.m.	Bn. relieved by 7th Camerons who "Trenches used CHAPEL ALLEY (up) DEVON LANE (down): DEVON LANE was now being in a condition to be used. The Camerons Hrs. did not take over from the Seaforth Hrs. the fore-trench North of the HULLUCH ROAD to the SOUTH END of the GAP (shown in sketch above). This was now added to the front held by the right Bn. of the Brigade, and was accordingly taken over by the 10th London who, took over ⅔ of it. STONE STREET was am it London who. Support trenches were held as formerly. Seaforth Hrs. took over Old German and Old British lines as formerly and commenced routine of keeping trenches in order. Diff	
C.2.	2/11/15		Bn. in local reserve. Heather Trench. Lt. B.G. Blackwood accidentally wounded in the leg by a bayonet. Diff	
C.2.	3/11/15		Bn. in local reserve. Heather Trench. Following Casualties of action 8/26 September published in Routine Orders: Wounded and invalided to Eng. land : 5 men. To m. Potts admitted to Hospital sick. Diff	
C.3.	7/11/15		Bn. relieved 7th Camerons the 7th line trenches. O.C. 7th Camerons reported the Germans on 6/3/11/15 had shelled his front line heavily inflicting about 30 casualties. O.C. 8th Devonshire decided to hold front line lightly. Two Companies were to be placed in front with 2 Platoons back in front line and two platoons in support line. Trenches used for relief were CHAPEL ALLEY (up) DEVON LANE (down). Bn Headquarters were as formerly in an old German dug-out about G. 11. D. 7. B. — Coys. were disposed as shown in following sketch.	

WAR DIARY

PLACE	DATE	TIME	SUMMARY OF EVENTS AND INFORMATION	REMARKS APPENDICES
Sector C2	4/1/15	pm		

[Sketch map showing trench positions with labels: BATTALION HEADQUARTERS, VERMELLES–HULLUCH RD, OLD GERMAN FRONT LINE, DUMP-BAC, LOOS–HAISNES, CHAPEL ALLEY, DEVON LANE, STONE LANE, QUARRIES, "A" Coy, "C" Coy, 2 Platoons "B" Coy, 2 Platoons "D" Coy, TO HULLUCH-1, Scale 1/10,000]

Relief had hardly been completed, when Germans started heavy artillery fire on our fire-trench. They flew in front trench from DEVON LANE to CHAPEL ALLEY, and the trench as such ceased to exist. The Commanding Officer himself was in the support trenches when the shelling was going on, and afterwards crawled along the support bit of the trench north of CHAPEL ALLEY also. The trench was completely blown in, in several places, and large

WAR DIARY

PLACE	DATE	TIME	SUMMARY OF EVENTS AND INFORMATION	REMARKS APPENDICES
C 2	4/11/15		Trenches filled up, almost to ground level. Sgt G.W. Harper and 1 man were wounded and 1 man killed. Telephonic communication - probably owing to the bad weather and falling in of the trenches - was disorganised and at the time it was impossible to communicate by telephone either with the Brigade, or with the Infantry. The C.O. despatched a runner to Brigade Headquarters stating the facts of the case, and particularly drawing attention strongly to the bad state of the telephone wires which were troubled over Knotted and obstructed jumpy everywhere in the trenches. The Infantry holding two front line trenches with the smallest number of men possible; and had moved their H.Q. of the machine guns into the support line. Informed was received from the Brigade confirming these arrangements, and notifying that the 75 capacities General would meet the C.O. in the right portion of the trench at E. The enemy shelling seemed to come on to the left portion of the trench from the N.E. Our heavy gun - 9.2" - fired in retaliation on the enemy trenches. Capt. G.R. Addison returned this day from leave for duty.	— DofI
C 2	5/11/15		Brigadier General inspected damages to the lines by enemy shell fire of yesterday. During the day much was done by units concerned to clear up tangle of telephone wires in the trenches and relay them in a more satisfactory way 4/11/15 to 5/11/15. Leave of absence granted to 6 N. Co's and men from 5/11/15 to 12/11/15.	DofI
C 2	6/11/15		Enemy shelling HQ quite so active during the night. Work of repairing front trenches carried on by a Coy last night. Our machine guns disposed Roman working parties. Nest of sniping wounding/waving periodic into enemy trenches.	DofI

WAR DIARY

PLACE	DATE	TIME	SUMMARY OF EVENTS AND INFORMATION	REMARKS APPENDICES
C2.	7/10/15	P.M.	2nd Batt. the relieved by 12th H.L.I. 8/46th Sy. Bde. There 10th H.L.I only placed this Coy. in trenches relieved by gallantforths, 1 Coy going into old German front line vacated by Camerons. Instructed to leave trenches by DEVON LANE — OLD GERMAN FRONT LINE — "WING'S WAY" and then proceed by PHILOSOPHE — LE SAULCHOY FM. — RED ROAD to NOEUX-LES-MINES. To Posts are Bells to there. As the night was very dark (Cap. left WING'S WAY (Communication trench S. of the HULLUCH ROAD) and proceeded down the road itself transport was shifted to NOEUX-LES-MINES during the day. Dist. Served from 26th Oct. to 7th Nov. Note reference to this period of occupation of the trenches the following calling for remark have been (1) The inclement nature of the weather conditions. The weather has the first day of entering the trenches, and remained seemingly bad throughout the entire period. (2) The amount of work requiring to be done to the sector entrusted to us (a) in the way of digging and improving trenches (b) repairing damage caused by weather and by shell-fire (c) Collecting enormous titles of military material lying about the trenches since battle of 25th September and subsequently (d) Burying dead. (3) The fact that the work of the officers and men had 20 enormous influence of trenches before.	C2. 1/40,000 Sheet 36 B.

WAR DIARY

PLACE	DATE	TIME	SUMMARY OF EVENTS AND INFORMATION	REMARKS APPENDICES
			(1) The fact that the Divisional Artillery were firing an especially aggressive program against the enemy, the weather conditions naturally told on the men themselves heavily. Owing to frost and in such wet and mud, and work of such kinds these conditions got got bad; and so many as the men were over and had to be evacuated to hospital. A great deal of our time, however, in the day of my Bde, and improving trenches; the lines of communication trenches were kept in repair; DEVON LANE towards the front was made "concrete" and other trenches widened and improved. Pumps and much scope was used to keep the trenches dry. On the 29.10.15 instructions were received from the "4th Inf Bde." regarding "collection and evacuation of stores, Ammunition, Equipment Etc." Limbs etc collected and placed in suitable stores; Ammunition issued daily and sent with Stores, Rifles, Equipment etc. were collected daily and sent with Ration Carts at night to — Bde. Salvage Coy. at VERMELLES. A considerable number of dead were buried. Officers and men differ down with wonderful cheerfulness to a somewhat still of — hardship in Trench Warfare; and by the use of the few facilities the most inexpensive experience of the discomfort and difficulty, and the most commendable steadiness under shell fire and the other dangers of trench—warfare. It has been noted above that there was a period of nuclear artillery aggressiveness. A copy of a letter from the 4th Corps, under cover of G. Letter from the 1st Division was forwarded to the unit on 28/10/15. The 4th Corps letter (H.R.S 425) pointed out that the state of the Ammunition supply and the number of guns available had now materially improved, and it was most necessary that advantage of these conditions should be taken to secure an absolute superiority as regards Artillery fire over the enemy, the relative conditions between ourselves and them were	

WAR DIARY

Place	Date	Summary of Events and Information	Remarks references appendices

Moeuvres 8/11/15

Prevailed as compared with last year. The actual form which the policy of enemy harassment on the enemy should take when he decided by Divisional Commander. The 15th Bn. both intended that the policy there laid down by the Brigade Commander would be vigorously pursued. As a result during this twelve hours of the occupation of the trenches there was repeated activity "frightfulness" by our artillery night and day. The enemies own reprisals by the enemy took on our front and different trenches, and it is indeed gratifying considering the amount of material flung over our lines were not heavier than they were; specially as the method of relieving the line kept the men in Trenches all the time. Casualties for the period were 1 Officer and 5 men killed, 3 Officers and 18 men wounded.
DWL

" 9/11/15

Bn. in billets :—
Leave of absence from 8th to 17th inst. granted to five NCOs and men.
DWL

" 10/11/15

Divisional Baths. 3 N.C.O's and 25 men reported from Hospital for duty. Sent home reserves from 15th Bn. re guard principles for doubtful trench area occupies by the Division.
Bn. in billets :— The following is an extract from Routine Orders of this date "The Commanding Officer has much pleasure in announcing that the following honours have recently been awarded :—
Croix-de-chevalier Legion d'Honneur to Capt. & Adjt. D.W.P. Craig
Croix-de-guerre to 15/5 A/Catm R. MacPhail "D" Coy

WAR DIARY

PLACE	DATE	TIME	SUMMARY OF EVENTS AND INFORMATION	REMARKS & APPENDICES
NOEUX-LES-MINES	10/11/15		"The Commanding Officer has much pleasure in announcing that the Distinguished Conduct Medal has been awarded to No 9971 Cpl. J. Dunlop "C" Coy." Following casualties of left 25% out 96 published 1 N.C.O and 5 men*1?	
"	11/11/15		Bn in Billets. No 5/9787 L/Cpl A Sutherland "D" Grades ammunition Oct 31; published as off the strength D.R.O.	
"	12/11/15		Bn in billets. Preparations made for proceeding to trenches on 13th. Daily leave of absence reported from 12th to 17th inst granted to Cpl Cups and man for 6 days on medical F/lough 17/11/15 Mr R Aichison reported from F. Base	
D.1.	13/11/15	8 a.m.	Bn. left NOEUX-LES-MINES and proceeded to Sector (D1) on left of Sector of 145th Inf. Bde.. Sector D1 extended from G.12. a.4.2 to G.11. B.9.5. The Black Watch (9th) went into trenches on our left relieving to G.5.D.1.3. Lt F.C. Shaw and 50 other ranks left at VERMELLES as permanent working party. Coys were arranged as follows :- "D" Coy on the Right – The French & Support trench "A" Coy on the left – " " " "C" Coy in the German Front line "B" Coy in Old British Front line 18. Heavy rainfall were in a very small dug - out in Old British front line !	

WAR DIARY

PLACE	DATE/TIME	SUMMARY OF EVENTS AND INFORMATION	REMARKS APPENDICES
D1	13/11/15	7th Cameron Hrs relieved Camerons behind 2 Coys in our British front line and support trenches 1 Coy in huts at PHILOSOPHE. 2 Coys in billets in VERMELLES. Following casualties of action 25 & 26. 6 N.C.O and 8 men.	D.W.P.
D1	14/11/15	Bn in trenches. Weather wet, and trenches cleaned and scraped.	D.W.P
D1	15/11/15	Bn in trenches. Sapa being dug out from front line — Heavy firing. Shelling of front and support lines — 4 men killed, 3 died of wounds, 6 men wounded.	D.W.P
NOYELLES	16/11/15 a.m.	Bn relieved by 2nd 7th Camerons and moved into Brigade Reserve at NOYELLES. During casualties: (2nd 7th included) killed in action 3 N.C.O's and 8 men. Wounded 6 N.C.O's, 2 F.K. Hartinger, F.K. Kennedy, 2t W.C. Cameron, 9th W.C. Cameron, 9th Maclean; 30 N.C.O's and 101 men. M/wound of 2t D.W.P.	D.W.P
"	17/11/15	Bn in billets bathing and cleaning up. Parties of 5 officers and 250 men on working parties from 5.15 p.m. The following order was published by the G.O. this day: "The Commanding Officer has much pleasure in congratulating all ranks on the good work done during the last tour of duty in the trenches. Under very trying conditions they have been continuously under shellfire, but the uncomplaining spirit, the cheerfulness and the eagerness of the officers and men to keep the new trenches in a fit state of repair give satisfaction to the Commanding Officer and the efforts which have been made this tour to make the trenches more comfortable and more safe than before has been an advantage to those following." Casualties of 25/26 Sept. 1 man missing & think off strength.	D.W.P
"	18/11/15	Bn in billets. Preparations made for relieving 7th Camerons in trenches on 19/11/15.	D.W.P

WAR DIARY

PLACE	DATE TIME	SUMMARY OF EVENTS AND INFORMATION	REMARKS APPENDICES
D1	19/11/15	Bn. relieved 7th Camerons in Sector D1. Coys. were disposed as follows:- "B" Coy. Right of the trench "C" Coy. Left of Fire trench - commanded by Lt. & 6 Nant - Capt. G.R. Anderson being invalided. "A" Coy. Rear Support Line "D" Coy. In trench Front Line. Heavy shelled "C" Coy. for about an hour. One shell landed in the trench killing one man, and wounding one man. D.W.P.J	
D1	20/11/15	Bn. in trenches. Wiring parties wired in front of "B" and "C" Coys.. Heavy shelled BRESLAU AVENUE Communication trench to front line, catching working party of "A" Coy about 10.30 p.m. and wounding 7 men. D.W.P.J	
D1	21/11/15	Bn. in trenches. Further wiring carried on. BRESLAU AVENUE improved along whole length. Home to C.O's received. D.W.P.J Party orders to-day about 599 men in trenches including specialists - 169 men in hospital.	
D1	22/11/15	Bn. relieved by 7th Camerons the proceeded into local reserve. D Coy remained in position. A, B, C Coys proceeded into billets in VERMELLES. D.W.P.J	
VERMEL-LES	23/11/15	Bn. in local Reserve. Lt. G. Blackwood invalided to England, and struck off the strength. D.W.P.J	
VERMEL-ES - VERQUIN	24/11/15 8 a.m	Bn. set forth the relieve by 6th Camerons. 45th Inf. Bde. - moved into billets in VERQUIN via NOYELLES - SAILLY LA BOURSE - VERQUIGNEUL - VERQUIN and took on billets vacated by 12th H.L.I.. Draft of 9 N.C.O.'s and 21 men joined battalion and were posted for duty to N.C.O.'s and 20 men rejoined the Bn. for duty. D.W.P.J	

WAR DIARY

PLACE	DATE	TIME	SUMMARY OF EVENTS AND INFORMATION	REMARKS APPENDICES
VERQUIN			Period of occupation of trenches 13/11/15 to 24/11/15. The features marking this period of occupation of the trenches have been (1) the continued bad weather, and great amount of work requiring to be done to trenches. (2) have marked heavy rifle to entrained approaches, relays of our divisional artillery (3) Difficulty of bringing up water and supplies. Difficulty of getting up supplies — the Medium Water Carts left NOYELLES at 4.15pm and carried supply of water Brigade Water Carts left NOYELLES at 5pm. The water was transferred to tanks, and to VERMELLES arriving there at 5pm. In the old Bristol trenches at 6.10 A.G.C. conveyed by tramway to a Dump 1 officer and 20 men to take the trolleys. The Battalion in reserve found 1 officer and 20 men to push the trolleys to the Dump. Ration Carts of battalion to D.1. Left NOYELLES at 5 pm arrived at VER-MELLES at 5.45. Any rations arrived at the Dump at 6.30pm at	
			— Rations for battalion in D.2 were drawn at 7.30pm, for one. (4) of Royal Reserve to in Old British line at 8.30pm. Wolf Tanks were emptied starting at 8.30pm. A second ration left NOYELLES at 7.45pm arrived tramway and at 8.30 pm and at Into Dump 9.15pm. This ration was left in reserve supply to draw in at discretion of units next day. The units mentioned being under of guard. The Bn. left behind a ration party of 20 men — 4 Lt Tully to trench railways to the Dump, & Lt. Duncan i/c fatigue detail or Brigade transport Officer in charge of these arrangements.	

WAR DIARY

PLACE	DATE TIME	SUMMARY OF EVENTS OR INFORMATION	REMARKS APPENDICES
		The arrangements were probably the best in the circumstances but left much to be desired. From the dump the materials had still to be carried a very long way to the front trenches and as it was impossible to deflect the CRE there, to provide any parties for both work and returns, parties for the latter were drawn from the Coy in BHQ British line. The working of the system at the Dump depended on the promptitude and punctuality of parties from different parties and in the condition of the trenches (dangerous in some places when it rained) arrangement working regularly. An effort was detected to last to keep the arrangement working by the OC in DI, as it happened there was only enough to keep the Dump supplied and occasional shelling. D.W.R. [?]
YPRAVIN	25/11/15	Day devoted to cleaning and flushing up. Measures of "stand pit" issued to Coy. No 370 by Cpl J. Ward replaced by B.G. Cm. & Inn the F.P. no 1. 2/Lt. J. Milne and 2/Lt B. Murray Henry Jones to be for duty are posted to D Coy respectively in moving force action of Sept 25/26 strict of the strength. D.W.R. [?]
"	26/11/15	On m shells, a ↔ B Coy at Corks at the Mine D.W.R. [?]

WAR DIARY

PLACE	DATE HOUR	SUMMARY OF EVENTS & INFORMATION	REMARKS & REFERENCES
VERDUN	27/11/15	Bn. in hutts. C. to D. Coys. at mine baths. Leave to U.K. granted to 5 N.C.O's and men. Divine Service.	DUTY
"	28/11/15	Divine Service.	DUTY
"	29/11/15 a.m.	Bn. in hutts.	
	2.30 pm	Croix-de-Guerre presented to Sgt. R. McPhail "D" Coy. by Major-General McCracken, the Bn. being paraded in the field behind the Château. Brigadier-General Scrase Dickens K.V.O. was present. Major-General McCracken explained that their decoration was granted by the French Government on a recognition of what Great Britain had done for France in the present great battles and informed his pleasure in presenting the medal to Sgt. McPhail as chosen to represent his gallant comrades to many of whom the supreme sacrifice of their lives was made. The following draft joined the Bn. today and two posted to "C" Coy. 1 N.C.O. and 26 men. 2/Lt. D.S. Inglefast having joined for duty from the base, to "A" Coy. for duty.	DUTY

Index..........................

SUBJECT.

8th Seaforths

C.W.
10 sheets

No.	Contents.	Date.
	December 1915.	

(63,965). Wt.15,820—176. 2000. 9/21. Gp.164. A.&E.W.

WAR DIARY

PLACE	DATE	TIME	SUMMARY OF EVENTS AND INFORMATION	REMARKS APPENDICES
VERQUIN	30/9/15		Bn. in billets. Instructions made for returning to trenches. 2 men missing since action of 25/26 Sept. Struck off strength. Lts. Miller and Synnman from R.H.S. joined Bn. for in situation french work. 2Lt. W.F. Ackaad joined forces for duty two day and was posted to "B" Coy.	
VERQUIN – VERMELLES	1/10/15	7.30 a.m.	Bn. left VERQUIN to proceed into local Reserve in Sector C (late Sector D) relieving 7th R.S.F., 45th Inf. Bde.. Two Coys. proceeded into old trenches at line "B" and "C", Coy, two Coys. "A" + "D" went into billets at PHILOSOPHE. Relief was completed about 12 noon. The following officers on this day attached to the Bn. for duty for R.M. Plumptre and 2 [Lts.] R. [Fraser?] [Traer?] 1/4th [Kent?] [Reserve?] [Watch?] transport bombing Rooms (August) at NOYELLES.	DWH
	5/10/15		Bn. in local Reserve. No 4983 Private A/Sgt. J. Gordon "C" Coy had his sentence of Sgt. R. Frau [re-]sentenced to 1 Year's imprisonment with Hard Labour "C" Coy confirmed by F.G.C.M. to Brig. General Wilkinson to 6 mths. Imp. with H.L. commuted by Brig. Genl. [Wilkinson]. Sentence suspended.	DWH
	7/10/15		Bn. in local Reserve. 2 N.C.O's and 3 men previously reported missing are now reported killed in action of 26 Sept. 25 by Central Information Bureau.	DWH
	8/10/15		Bn. relieved 7th Cameron Hrs in C.1. This sector runs Eastwards from about G.12.a.9.4. to about G.11.B.9.5. B and C moved	

WAR DIARY

PLACE	DATE	TIME	SUMMARY OF EVENTS AND INFORMATION	REMARKS APPENDICES
D 1	4/7/15		In old front line, "A" and "D" Coys being in support and reserve. Team of officers W.R. praided to S.N. Cos and men.	Diary
"	5/7/15		Bn in front trenches.	Diary
"	6/7/15		Bn in front trenches.	Diary
NOYELLES	7/7/15		7th Cameron Hrs relieved Bn in front trenches. Bn. moved back into bivouac Reserve NOYELLES. Brig Gen E. Wayne having orders for duty to forces to "A" Coy.	Diary
"	8/7/15		Bn in bivouac Reserve washing etc. No 5/6635 Pte A. Stephens "B" Coy sentenced by F.G.C.M. to 9 mths Imprisonment H.L. for (1) making rush by attempting to sell his clothing (2) Insubordinate language to two Superior Officers (3) Disobeying a lawful command given by two Superior Officers. Sentence confirmed and suspended by Brig-Genl H.C. Wilkinson M.V.O. No 5/6502 Pte J. Graham sentenced by F.G.C.M. to 84 days F.P. No1 for (1) being concerned in making away with clothing (2) losing by neglect his Govt equipment M.V.O. Diary	
"	9/7/15		Bn in Brigade Reserve.	Staff
"	10/7/15		Bn in Brigade Reserve — arrangements made for relieving 7th Camerons in D 1.	Diary

WAR DIARY

PLACE	DATE	TIME	SUMMARY OF EVENTS AND INFORMATION	REMARKS APPENDICES
D1	11/12/15		Bn. relieved 1st Camerons in D.1. Coys. were disposed as follows:— "D" Coy. Right front Coy. "A" Coy. Left " "B" Coy. Support Coy. "C" Coy. Reserve Coy. 1 man missing since we were left trench — strength	Duty
D1	12/12/15		Bn. in front line D.1. Draft of 4 N.C.O's and 50 men joined at NOYELLES that detached day, 1 N.C.O. and 15 men also detained who returned from Divisional Base. 4 N.C.O's and 15 men joined this day for duty. 1/Lt H.D. Holder joined this day for duty.	Duty
D1	13/12/15		Bn. in front line. Preparations made for relief by 17th London Regt. on 14/12/15. 1 man killed by a sniper of "D" Coy. — 1st casualty of the three days.	Duty
D1 — ALLOUAGNE	14/12/15		Bn. relieved by 17th London Regiment. Bren boots were landed over and French stoves. Relief commenced 7.15 a.m. Brigade transport left NOYELLES at 10 a.m. with Lt S.T. Duncan S/Lt and proceeded to ALLOUAGNE via BETHUNE and CHOCQUES. Coys. breakfasted at PHILOSOPHE and proceeded to NOEUX-LES-MINES where they entrained for LILLERS, from which they afterwards	

WAR DIARY

PLACE	DATE	TIME	SUMMARY OF EVENTS AND INFORMATION	REMARKS APPENDICES
			Marched to billets at ALLOUAGNE.	
ALLOUAGNE	16/12/15		Staff
			On in billets in Corps Reserve — ALLOUAGNE. Day devoted to cleaning up of men — clothing, equipment, and arms; inspection of kits, emergency rations; small helmets and cleaning of grenades and ammunition. Bn. will send the following journal to courses during period in Corps Reserve.	
			(1) 1st Army Officers Training School GOSNAY	
			1 Junior Officer for periods Dec. 16 to 21; Dec. 23 to 30; Jan 3 to 8; Jan. 10 to 15.	
			(2) M.G. School GOSNAY.	
			5 Officer + other ranks for periods Dec. 16 to 24; Dec. 26 to Jan. 4; Jan. 4 to Jan 13.	
			(3) French Mortar School GOSNAY.	
			2 other ranks for periods Dec. 16 to 21; Dec. 21 to 24.	
			2 other ranks + 1 officer for periods Dec. 27 to 30; Jan 2 to 5.	
			2 other ranks for periods Jan 5 to 8; Jan 8 to 11.	
			(4) Grenadier School at ALLOUAGNE. Since 4/10/15 Arrangements have been carried on continuously — 1 officer and 16 other ranks have proceeded every 4 days to Brigade Bombing School Officer Bn. HH Dva.	
			(5) Signal School. Bns. HH Dva. Dec. 16 to Dec. 22	
			1 officer for period	

WAR DIARY

PLACE	DATE TIME	SUMMARY OF EVENTS AND INFORMATION	REMARKS APPENDICES
		1 Sgt. and 3 weeks in Equitus from Dec. 16 to Dec. 30. 1 Cpl. and 3 weeks course Equitus from Jan. 2 to 14. (c) Brigade Signal School. Brigade Arrangements. The following training is arranged for the Battalion Dec. 16th to 22nd – Platoon Training Dec. 23rd to Jan. 5th – Company Training Jan. 6th to January 31st – Battalion Training. DsDS	
ALLOUAGNE	1/1/15	Bn. in billets cleaning up. Lt J.N. Rees and 6 Platoon Officers course. 2 NCO's and 13 men attached to "70" Coy R.E. DsDS	
"	11/1/15	Bn. in billets. Cleaning up. "D" Coy and "C" Coy at baths MARLES-LES-MINES. 2 men reported by Aerial Information Bureau as buried one at LOOS, one at BRUSSELS 5 men reported killed on Sept 25th.	
"	12/1/15	Platoon & Specialist training and Courses. Draft arrived for half Bn of 6 N.C.O's and 43 men A & B Coys. at baths. MARLES - LES - MINES 3 N.C.O's and 7 men. Ammunition reduced to 120 rounds carried on the man. Capt. G.R. Anderson reported this day for duty and was posted to "D" Coy. Leave of absence H.U.K. granted to Pte W.J. Walters + 11 other ranks Sept.	

WAR DIARY

PLACE	DATE	TIME	SUMMARY OF EVENTS AND INFORMATION	REMARKS APPENDICES
ALLOUAGNE	19/12/15	—	Platoon and Specialist training. Inspection of billets by Commanding Officer. Divine Service. Lt. C. G. Haynes takes over duties of Bn. M.G. Officer.	DWT
"	20/12/15		Platoon and Specialist Training Courses. Training of war by Central Information Bureau. 1 N.C.O. and 5 men reported prisoners of war. 1 N.C.O. and 2 men left duty struck off strength missing since action of 25th Sept.	DWT
"	21/12/15		Platoon and Specialist Training Courses. Lecture by Adj. Major on Trench Duties. 1 N.C.O. struck off strength missing since Sept 25. 3 men reported prisoners of war. 3 N.C.O. and 2 men from 27/9/15 to 2/12/15. Leave of absence granted to F.G.Cpl. to 56 days F.P. Pollocks L/Cpl. W. Phillips "B" Coy. sentenced by F.G.C.M. DWT to 56 days F.P. for sentence confirmed by Lt-Col. J.W. Sandilands. DWT	DWT
"	22/12/15		Platoon and Specialist training Courses. Leave of absence granted to K/Cpl. D.E. Thinkee from 23/9/15 to 3/1/16.	DWT
"	23/12/15		Company and Specialist training Courses. Capt. C.C. Forsyth took over Command of Battalion in absence of Lt.Col. J.F. Hepdee.	DWT
"	24/12/15		Company and Specialist training Courses. 1 N.C.O. and 20 men proceeded to BETHUNE on loading duties.	DWT

WAR DIARY

PLACE	DATE	TIME	SUMMARY OF EVENTS AND INFORMATION	REMARKS APPENDICES
ALLOUAGNE	18/12/15	9.15am	Church of England Service. General Holiday	
"	26/12/15		Lt. Col. N.A. Thomson have rejoined for duty resumes command of the Battalion. Captain [illegible] R. Jackson 2nd. in Command. The Commanding Officer DW R	Staff
"	27/12/15		Company and Specialist Training Harness. 6 men missing since 25th inst. Since 3 men sufficiently reported missing from the Someny(?) & referred through Central Information Bureau.	DW R
"	28/12/15		Company and Specialist Training Harness	DW R
"	29/12/15		Company and Specialist Training Harness. S/Sjt. Pte (L/Cpl) J. Henderson sentenced by F.G.C.M. to 30 days' imprisonment H.L. for Drunkenness. Sentence confirmed by Lt Col J.W. Swithenbank, Acting Brigadier, and commuted to 28 days F.P. No. 1. Lt. G.W. Duncan appointed Acting Adjutant during the absence of Capt D.W.P. Strang.	DW R
"	30/12/15		Company and Specialist Training Harness. Leave of absence granted to Capt S. Robinson, 2/Lt. S.J. Newell, 2/Lt. W. Murray, 2/Lt. K. Robertson and 15 other ranks. 2/Lt. G. Milne attended aerodrome in the absence of Capt K. Robertson Transport Officer, 2/Lt. W.H. Graham took over duties of acting Transport Officer	

WAR DIARY

PLACE	DATE	TIME	SUMMARY OF EVENTS AND INFORMATION	REMARKS APPENDICES
ALLOUAGNE	24/10/15		Company and Specialist training. 2/Lieut H.N. Potter reported to England on 21/10/15	[signature]

Army Form C. 2118

WAR DIARY
or
INTELLIGENCE SUMMARY
(Erase heading not required.)

Place	Date	Hour	Summary of Events and Information	Remarks and references to Appendices

Instructions regarding War Diaries and Intelligence Summaries are contained in F. S. Regs., Part II. and the Staff Manual respectively. Title Pages will be prepared in manuscript.

1/10,000 2nd edition
Sheet 36c N.W.3
Permanent Station No. 3.

GERMAN LINES
NORTHERN SAP
SOUTHERN SAP
D COY
SAP 45
A COY
SIXTH AVENUE
B "COY"
18
WAY ALLEY
A
ESSEX LANE
C
VENDIN ALLEY
BUS GARREE
"C" COY
HD QRS
LONE TREE
ENGINEERS DUMP
RATION DUMP
46th Brigade

Army Form C. 2118

WAR DIARY
or
INTELLIGENCE SUMMARY
[Erase heading not required]

Instructions regarding War Diaries and Intelligence Summaries are in F.S. Regs., Part II. and the Staff Manual respectively. Title pages will be prepared in Manuscript.

Place	Date	Hour	Summary of Events and Information	Remarks and References to Appendices
ALLOUAGNE	1/1/16	-	New Years Day. This day was observed as a holiday. Coy. General M.G. Milburn M.V.O. Cmdg. 19th Inf. Bde. visited Companies at dinner.	(Ans)
"	2/1/16	-	Divine Service was held in divisional Recreation room. O.C.s divine Service the Commanding Officer inspected Company billets.	(Ans)
"	3/1/16	-	Company training was carried out including Musketry, rapid loading & unloading. Attack of the attack. 10 O.R. were reported invalided to England & struck off the Okey H. accordingly. On man Pte. J.J. Bell ("D" Coy) was taken prisoner of war at Krupp. Leigrette Dopensen dates 6th/15 - Lieut.s Pte. Shaw, Mr. Darling & Mr. Taylor & 109 O.R. were granted leave to U.K. from 4th inst. to 12th inst.	(Ans)
"	4/1/16	-	Company training was carried out. Preparations made for the Battalion to take part in a divisional Route March Commencing 5th inst.	(Ans)
"	5/1/16	-	The Battn. marched from Allouagne at 9.5am in the order A.B.C.D. Coys. M.G.Section. Transport marched to 2 Echelon. "A" & "B" – "A" echelon consisted of 4 Machine Gun	

WAR DIARY OR INTELLIGENCE SUMMARY

[Erase heading not required]

Place	Date	Hour	Summary of Events and Information	Remarks and references to Appendices
			Walker Cst	
ALLOUAGNE	5/4/16	9am	Limbers, 2 S.A.A. Carts & 1 Water Cart – this echelon marched immediately behind the Battalion – "B" echelon consisted of 4 travelling Kitchens, Mess Cart, 2 S.A.A. Limbers & Mob. Cart. This echelon marched under the Brigade Transport Officer, Lieut. P. Cairn, 9th Black Watch. The route followed was via BORBORE – ECQUEDECQUES – LIERES – AUCHY-AU-BOIS	
		3pm	About 3pm on arrival at RELY billet orders were received that the Battn. would billet here. By 4.30pm all men were in billets. Snd	
RELY	6/4/16	12.5am	Orders were received that the 15th Division was ordered to prepare a position for their purposes on high ground between the rivers Lys and A.D. from DOHEME to AUDINEIUN	
RELY	6/4/16		That the Division would advance in three columns, heads to arrive at billets upon the river Lys at DELETTE, COYECQUE & DENNEBROEUCQ at 11am. That the Brigade Group would form the Centre Column.	
RELY	6/4/16	7.30am	The S.D. Leafs of the Battn. marched from RELY at 7.30am in the order D.C.B.A. Coys. M.G. Section. The transport marched in the same array as the previous day.	

Army Form C 2118

Instructions regarding War Diaries
and Intelligence Summaries are in
F.S. Regs, Part II and the Staff
Manual Respectively. Title pages
will be prepared in Manuscript.

WAR DIARY
or
INTELLIGENCE SUMMARY
[Erase heading not required]

Place	Date	Hour	Summary of Events and Information	Remarks & References to Appendices
	6/1/16		Passed the starting point which was the road junction just west of the C in CUINCHY at 9.5 a.m. The route followed was FRUY - ST. JULIEN - BONY - PETIGNY - COYECQUE.	
	6/1/16	2.30pm	At 2.30pm orders were received that the 44th Brigade Group would march back to the billeting area occupied by them the previous night, the 8th Seaforth H'ders accordingly marched back to RELY & reached their billets of the previous night by 6.30pm.	
RELY	6/1/16	10.30pm	Orders were received that the 15th Division would march at the following morning to the LILLERS billeting area and that 44th Brigade Group would march as part of an Advanced Guard to the Division. That the route to be followed was AUCHY AU BOIS - BELLERY - HURIONVILLE - BURBURE. It was also notified for information that the Exercise would finish as troops passed the crossroads 1/3 mile S of Second Ave in AUCHY AU BOIS.	

Instructions regarding War Diaries
and Intelligence Summaries are in
F.S. Regs., Part II. and the Staff
Manual respectively. Title pages
will be prepared in manuscript.

WAR DIARY
or
INTELLIGENCE SUMMARY
[Erase heading not required]

Army Form C. 2118.

Place	Date	Hour	Summary of Events and Information	Remarks & References to Appendices
			and that rifts passing that point to protect the armies need to take, the troops motoring straight to their respective billets which they had left on the 5th inst.	
RELY	7/1/16	8.30am	The 5th Seaforth Hdrs marched from RELY at 8.30am in the order B,C,D,A. Coys. M.G. Section passed the starting point at 8.50am - the Battn then marched straight back to ALLOUAGNE on the route previously ordered & arrived in their billets about 1pm. During the whole of the Exercise the troops used their HAZEBROCK SHEET 5A.	
ALLOUAGNE	8/1/16		Company training. Lieut W. Murray & Lieut. J.M. Cameron & O.R. proceeded on a course of instruction in machine gun at GOSNAY.	
"	9/1/16		Rum Issues. Two left in divisional Recreation Room at 9.45am rafts division service. The Company billets were inspected by the Commanding Officer.	
"	10/1/16		Company training. The Battn. had the use of the Baths at MARLES-LES-MINES.	

Instructions regarding War Diaries
and Intelligence Summaries are in
F.S. Regs., Part II and the Staff
Manual respectively. Title pages
will be prepared in manuscript.

WAR DIARY
or
INTELLIGENCE SUMMARY
(Erase heading not required)

Army Form C. 2118

PLACE	DATE	HOUR	SUMMARY OF EVENTS and INFORMATION	Remarks and References to Appendices
ALLOUAGNE	11/1/16		Company training – 9 O.R. having been invalided to England were struck off the strength of the battalion.	
	12/1/16		Company training – Kit inspection of all companies by the Commanding Officer – Capt. G. Murray (M.C.) Lieut. J.C. Duncan & 17 O.R. were granted leave to United Kingdom	
"	13/1/16	-	Company training & general cleaning up of billets in view of returning to the trenches that	
	14/1/16	-	The Battn. marched from ALLOUAGNE to LILLERS STATION at 7.30am in to order C.O. A. B. Coy.	
			of LILLERS the Battn entrained for NOEUX-LES-MINES arriving there at 10.45am –	
			On arrival at NOEUX-LES-MINES the Battn was billeted & dinners were issued, the travelling kitchens having arrived at about 1pm. having come by road from ALLOUAGNE	
			At 2.45pm the Battn. moves off by Companies to relieve the 2nd Royal Sussex Regt	
			in that part of the 1st Bde section from H.31.C.6.9. to the left at H.25.a.5.2.	
			Companies were met by Guides at the level crossing PHILOSOPHE at 5pm & proceeded to the trenches via main LENS-BETHUNE road. The relief was completed by 10pm.	

Instructions regarding War Diaries
and Intelligence Summaries are in
F.S. Regs., Part II and the Staff
Manual respectively. Title pages
will be prepared in manuscript.

WAR DIARY
or
INTELLIGENCE SUMMARY
[Erase heading not required]

Army Form C. 2118

Place	Date Hour	Summary of Events and Information	Remarks & references to Appendices
	14/9/16	The disposition of companies being as follows - Officers line "B" - right firing line "A" Coy. Support line "D" Coy. 1st line transport & Quartermasters stores having proceeded by road were billets in MAZINGARBE. In this sector rations parties (in petrol tins) are brought up main LENS-BETHUNE road to LOOS & dumped at Batn Headquarters which are in LOOS in a cellar on the LOOS-HULLUCH road. Ration parties being sent down from trenches consisting of 25 men per Company. Capt G.R. Andrews was attached to 4th Brigade Intelligence Office - Machine guns were brought into potentially the line under orders issued by the Brigade Machine gun Officer.	
Brigade H.Q. 15/9/16		The front line was shelled intermittently all day. "D"Coy of 6th Royal Irish Regiment was attached to the Batt. to instruct on Y1 Platoon was sent to each Coy. During the night of 15th/16th the line held by 9th Hepwth Brigade was reorganised & the front of the line now held by 8th Seaforth Htdrs. extends from POSEN ALLEY (inclusive) to BOYAU-DES-ANGLAIS.	

WAR DIARY
or
INTELLIGENCE SUMMARY
(Erase heading not required)

Army Form C. 2118

Intelligence Summaries are in
P.S. Regs. Part II and the Staff
Manual respectively. Title pages
will be prepared in Manuscript.

Place	Date	Hour	Summary of Events and Information	Remarks and references to Appendices
Putisle Aubectin	16/1/16		Battn in trenches. The day passed quietly except for some slight shelling of the front line trenches & also LOOS. 1 man of "B" Coy was killed – Lieut. K. Smith & 5 OR were wounded.	
			Granted Leave to United Kingdom.	
"	17/1/16		Battn in trenches – little activity. 1 man of "C" Coy killed with shrapnel. 1 wounded	
"	18/1/16		Battn in trenches – 1 wounded	
"	19/1/16		Battn in trenches.	
"	20/1/16		Battn in trenches – during the night the Battn were relieved by 10th Gordon Hldrs – the relief was commenced at 6.30pm but owing to 2 platoons 10th Gordon Hldrs having lost their way, was not complete until 12.45 am next morning – on relief Companies moved back to Brigade Reserve in Lensh Avenue (old German front line – the disposition of Companies was as follows from right to left – "D" Coy with 2 platoons in LENS ROAD REDOUBT – 1 platoon in 65 METRE POINT REDOUBT, "C" Coy in 10th Avenue – "A" Coy in 10th Avenue. 1 platoon in NORTHERN SAP REDOUBT	

WAR DIARY
or
INTELLIGENCE SUMMARY
[Erase heading not required]

War Diaries and Intelligence Summaries are in F.S. Regs. Part II and the Staff Manual respectively. Title pages will be prepared in Manuscript.

Place	Date	Hour	Summary of Events and Information	Remarks and References to Appendices
	20/4/16		"B" Coy in 10th Avenue. Battn Headquarters were in a small kench off Pont Street. Rations were brought up by the trench railway from Victoria Station. (initialled)	
10th Avenue	21/4/16		Battn in Brigade Reserve. – At 10 men were working at night under Brigade arrangements. boys they were infantry reported batallion from leave (initialled)	
	22/4/16		Battn in Brigade Reserve. Working parties of 400 men were again found by the Battn. (initialled)	
"	23/4/16		Battn in Brigade Reserve. At 4.30pm Companies moved off from "Tenth Avenue" to relieve Companies of 1st Cameron Highrs in the Right Subsection of the Ponts 14 bis sector. Companies were disposed as follow:— B Coy right of firing line. C Coy left of firing line D Coy in support of ballaro in Loos A Coy in Reserve in Gun Alley. The limits of the front held by the battalion were the Loos — St Laurent Road (inclusive) to Belau Des Air Glas (inclusive)	

Instructions regarding War Diaries and Intelligence Summaries are in F. S. Regs., Part II and the Staff Manual Respectively - Title pages will be prepared in Manuscript.

WAR DIARY or INTELLIGENCE SUMMARY

Army Form C. 2118

[Erase heading not required.]

PLACE	DATE	HOUR	SUMMARY OF EVENTS AND INFORMATION	Remarks and References to Appendices

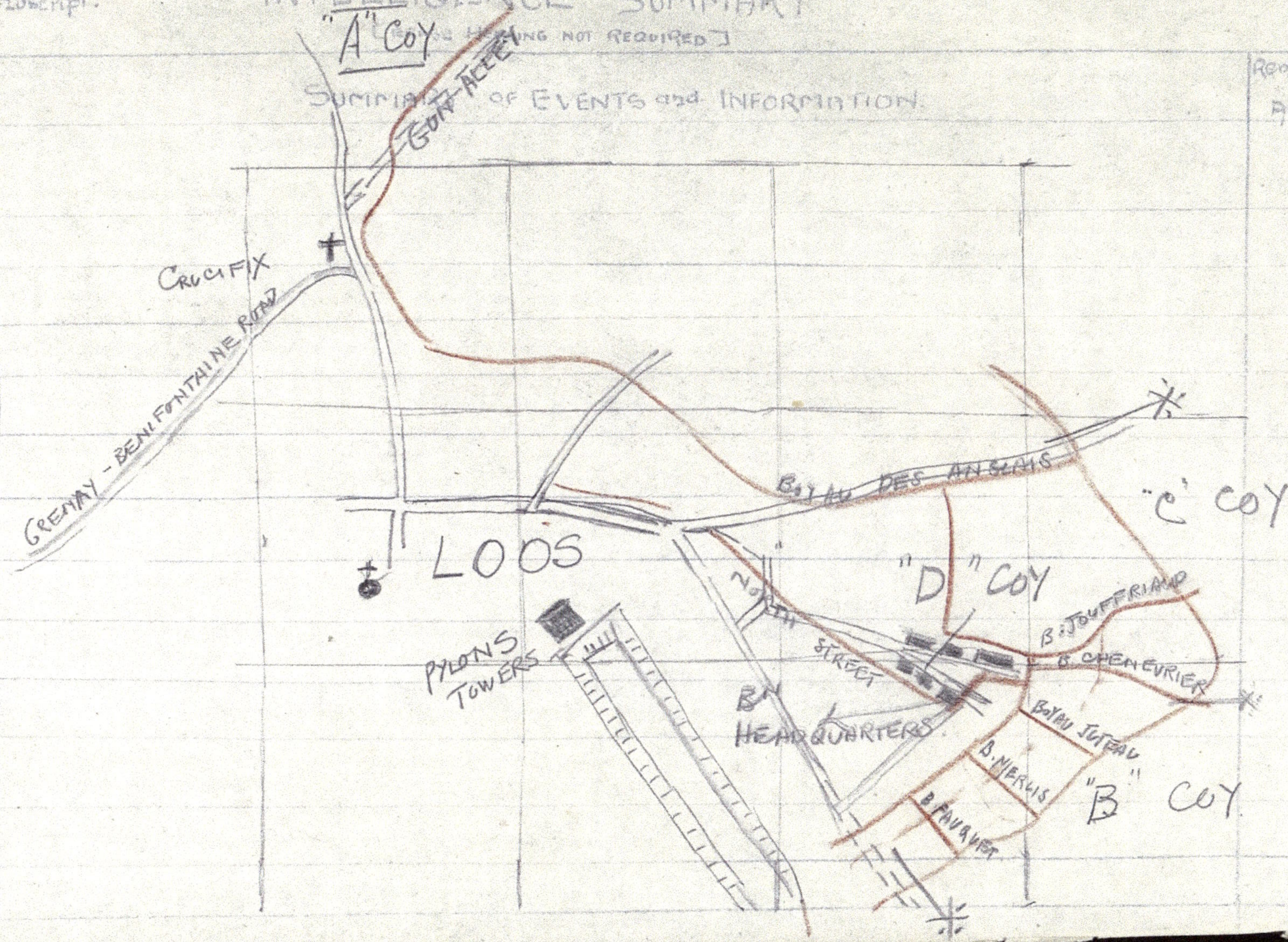

"A" COY
GUN ALLEY
CRUCIFIX
GRENAY - BENIFONTAINE ROAD
LOOS
BOYAU DES ANGLAIS
"C" COY
"D" COY
NORTH STREET
PYLONS TOWERS
Bn HEADQUARTERS
B. JOUFFRIAND
B. CHENEVRIER
BOYAU JUTEAU
B. MERLIS
B. FAUQUET
"B" COY

Army Form C 2118

WAR DIARY
or
INTELLIGENCE SUMMARY
[Erase heading not required]

Instructions regarding War Diaries and Intelligence Summaries are in F.S. Regs., Part II and the Staff Manual respectively. Title Pages will be prepared in manuscript.

Place	Date	Hour	Summary of Events and Information	Remarks & References to Appendices
RIGHT SUB-SECTION — PUITS XIV BIS SECTION	24/1/16		Under the arrangement "A" Coy in case of attack under take a very considerable time to man up to the front trenches. OC 7th [Queens] thinks it out that the arrangement was not intended to be permanent; but where new Left & new Russian trenches & Reply Completion of Zoos are completed, these ought to be occupied. Reply Completion 4 p.m. Four of Princes the Day granted to left of Grasfond & 2 Bn Princes and of other Ports to proceed to the N.R. 1 Of and 14 men transferred to 273rd (Annesley/Coy) R.E. Bn.[?]	
			Br in Right Sub-Section HULLUCH SECTION. Trenches quiet. Heavy artillery active. 9mm at 200S.	
	25/1/16		Bn in Left Sub-Section HULLUCH SECTION. Letter received from Brigadier General Welman, pointing out that	

Army Form C. 2118

WAR DIARY
or
INTELLIGENCE SUMMARY

[Erase heading not required]

Instructions regarding War Diaries and Intelligence Summaries are contained in F.S. Regs, Part II and the Staff Manual respectively. Title pages will be prepared in manuscript.

Place	Date	Hour	Summary of Events and Information	Remarks & References to Appendices
	Jan.		On hearing the Divn's birthday being might attempt an infantry attack against LOOS. Officer Commanding decided to put "D" Coy into support trenches E of LOOS and to bring up "A" Coy from GUN ALLEY into the cellars at LOOS. This was done during the night, and passed quietly.	
RIGHT SUB-SECTION	6/1/16	3 am	At this time Capt. E.K.O FERGUSSON Commanding B Coy S/O to fact Hs accompanied by Major R. Page, Royal Irish (attached) was walking along the fire trench to make sure that connection with Loodon Regiment on the right was fully established. The Commanding Officer regrets to record that just when they got across the LOOS – ST LAURENT ROAD these two officers were killed by shell-fire. Lt. W. Murray took over Command of "B" Coy S/O to fact Hs.	
			At dawn the barrier in the LOOS – ST LAURENT ROAD WORKS show very little damage that could not be repaired in daylight.	

Army Form C. 2118

WAR DIARY
or
INTELLIGENCE SUMMARY
[Erase heading not required]

Instructions regarding War Diaries and Intelligence Summaries are in F.S. Regs, Part II and the Staff Manual Respectively. Title Pages will be prepared in manuscript.

Place	Date	Hour	Summary of Events and Information	Remarks + References to Appendices
			During the day D. Cy. were withdrawn from the trenches back into cellars.	
		5:15pm	"A" & "C" O.T.B. left the LEVEL CROSSING PHILOSOPHE to relieve 8th Seaforth. "B" & "D" Pltn. occupied the line with R.B.Cy. and had to D	
			Cy. in cellars. Ammunition dumps near for relief **NORTH STREET**. Bryant, Tuteau, Chenevrier, Jouffriaud. Relief complete about 11pm.	
			Enemy artillery had shelled LOOS heavily during the day. Casualties Gt. Yeoman	
			On relief 8th Seaforth Bn. moved into Divisional Reserve at NOEUX - LES - MINES being billeted in ROUTE NATIONALE. Orders were received by O.C. Cys. at Advanced Brigade Report Centre 200 yds E of LEVEL CROSSING PHILOSOPHE that Bn. would proceed totally in advance to Nine at Point Idea. Bn. in Divisional Reserve had	
NOEUX-LES-MINES	29/4/16	Noon	Capt. E.K.G. Fergusson buried in the cemetery NOEUX-LES-MINES in presence of the C.O., other officers of the Bn. and B. Cy. Brigadier-General Graham Watkinson	

WAR DIARY
or
INTELLIGENCE SUMMARY
(Erase heading not required.)

Army Form C. 2118

Instructions regarding War Diaries and Intelligence Summaries are contained in F.S. Regs., Part II. and the Staff Manual respectively. Title Pages will be prepared in manuscript.

Place	Date	Hour	Summary of Events and Information	Remarks and references to Appendices
NOEUX-LES-MINES	29/1/16	7.25 pm	Attended the Funeral. Orders for the Battalion to be in readiness to move cancelled by 44th Brigade.	
"	28/1/16		New B.M. 6.23 O.R. still arrived 26/1/16 to-day joined H.Qrs to which they were posted. Bn. in Divisional Reserve :—	Draft
"		11 am	44th Brigade wire S.C. 445 received ordering the Battalion to stand-to in billets in readiness to move at once if required. Major J. E. Hart and 10 O.R. granted leave this day to proceed to the U.K. Leave of absence being also granted to 2/Lt S.M. Comrack.	Draft
"	29/1/16		Bn. in billets. Day spent in use of Divisional Bath House. Staff of 10 men joined the Battalion this day; 19 men also reported from 15th Infantry Base Depot.	Draft
"	30/1/16		Bn. in billets. Divine Service held. Company Commanders and Supplying Officer reconnoitred RIGHT SUB-SECTION, MUNICH, to be taken over from 13 Bn. Royal Scots.	Draft Draft
"	31/1/16		Bn. in billets. Day spent in preparation for move into the trenches on night 31st/2nd Feby.	Draft

8th Seaforths
Vol 1
15 Div

8.W
15.Jhels

WAR DIARY
or
INTELLIGENCE SUMMARY
(Erase heading not required.)

Army Form C. 2118

Place	Date	Hour	Summary of Events and Information	Remarks and references to Appendices
NOEUX-LES-MINES	1/2/16	1.45 pm	Bath left NOEUX-LES-MINES to relieve 13th Royal Scots in right Sub-Section, HULLUCH SECTION. Order of March A.B.D Coys.	
		3.30 pm	Guide of 13th Royal Scots met A.B.D Coys at LEVEL CROSSING PHILOSOPHE and conducted them by VERMELLES and communication trenches South of the VERMELLES - HULLUCH ROAD to the front line	
		4.45 pm	"C" Coy having moved independently to PHILOSOPHE not guided at the X-roads, but moved by LENS-BETHUNE ROAD, and thence from a point about 100 yds beyond the LEVEL CROSSING PHILOSOPHE, across the open in a N.E direction to TENTH AVENUE (former German front line) from a point about 200 yds E. of BOIS CARREE to a point about 100 yds E of LONE TREE, where they relieved 45th Brigade permanent Working Party, and came into Bn. Reserve.

Bn. Headquarters were at G.17.D.2.4. (Reference Trench map Sh^t N.W.3 Provisional Edition No 3) 10,000

Bn. Transport remained at NOEUX-LES-MINES
Bn. Bn. Stores were moved to MALIN GARBE

The front taken over from the 13th Royal Scots extended from VENDIN ALLEY inclusive to SIXTH AVENUE inclusive.
Coys held the line as follows:—
"A" Coy. Right of the Group line from VENDIN ALLEY (inclusive) to HOLLY LANE (m- chaux)
"D" Coy. left of the group line from ABBEY LANE (exclusive) to SIXTH AVENUE (exclusive)
"B" Coy. Support line from VENDIN ALLEY (inclusive) to SIXTH AVENUE (in the line)
"C" Coy in reserve in TENTH AVENUE
Scheme of relief in accordance with 44th Brigade Scheme was carried out | |

WAR DIARY or INTELLIGENCE SUMMARY

Army Form C. 2118

Place	Date	Hour	Summary of Events and Information	Remarks and references to Appendices
TRENCHES	2/12/16		Bn. in trenches. Enemy moderately active. Casualties 1 man killed and 3 wounded.	
"	3/12/16		Bn. in trenches. Enemy artillery active. Casualties 4 men wounded, and 1 man died of wounds. Relieved in the evening by Princess of Wales Support Trench. Came into Bn. H.Q. 40,00 Sheet 36 c. Bivouac Trench. Came into Bn. H.Q. 40,00 Sheet 36c N.W. 3 Section 6; also 40,00 Sheet 36 c. D.R.Y	
"	4/12/16		Bn. in trenches. Day passed fairly quietly. Three men wounded. In the evening the Bn. was relieved by the 4th Black Watch. H.Q. moved back into Brigade Support in TENTH AVENUE and Headquarters at G.17.B.7.6.	
"	5/12/16		Bn. in Brigade Support. ESSEX LANE defences for 400 yds. from SUPPORT LINE westwards. HAY ALLEY defences for 400 yds. from SUPPORT LINE eastwards. Also at VENDIN ALLEY Point re-arranged. 44.1.B / 5.105 — were this day received giving 4th Corps No. 1465.G. which states that "there is reason to believe that in the event of an East wind, seeming either for a period of this or four days, as is often the case at this time of the year, the enemy contemplate a gas attack on the front now occupied by the Lt. Corps." Casualties NIL.	

Army Form C. 2118

WAR DIARY
or
INTELLIGENCE SUMMARY

Army Form C. 2118.

Place	Date	Hour	Summary of Events and Information	Remarks and references to Appendices
TRENCHES	5/2/16		44th I.B. B.M. 735 was also received pointing out that considerable activity of the enemy reported at present might be the prelude to an attack at night although seen that the enemy was strengthening his line, but in the circumstances firing of the line was required, and patrolling with a view to finding out what the enemy was doing and disturbing him. Four other ranks were this day reported as wounded (slight), and were struck off the strength. Five men of the German patrol received slight sniper/infantry wounds. Two men and 1 Cpl and 1 man and were killed. Div. Routine Orders contained the following :— The following is an extract from the supplement to the London Gazette dated 14th January 1916 and is published for information :— "His Majesty the King has been graciously pleased to approve of the undermentioned rewards and awards for distinguished service in the field, with effect from 1st January 1916 inclusive. MILITARY CROSS. Captain Duncan William Park Strang. DISTINGUISHED CONDUCT MEDAL. 3/3496 C.S.M. W.A. Cunne "B" Coy 3/1575 A/C.S.M. R. McPhail "D" Coy 5/2700 Pte. F. McElone "A" Coy	

WAR DIARY
or
INTELLIGENCE SUMMARY
(Erase heading not required.)

Army Form C. 2118.

Place	Date	Hour	Summary of Events and Information	Remarks and references to Appendices
	5/1/16		"The following is an extract from the Supplement to the London Gazette, dated 1st January 1916 — Published for Information. MENTIONED IN DESPATCHES. Temporary Lieut-Col N.A. Thomson Major F.S. Bomber Captain D.W.P. Thing Infantry Capt. E.K.O. Ingram R/9244 C.S.M. A.H. Moor "C" Coy S/2783 A/Sgt G. Edwards "D" Coy S/3633 A/Sgt J.O'Donnell "D" Coy S/1476 A/Sgt M. Sydenham "A" Coy STAFF	
TRENCHES	6/1/16		Bn. in Brigade Support. HAY ALLEY deepened to 7 feet along whole length; also ESSEX LANE carrying parties provided for R.E. 1st Lt Thomas and this O.R. proceeded to GORNAY on M.G. Course. Other men reported invalided to England. STAFF	
TRENCHES	7/1/16	5 p.m.	Bn. relieved 9th R.Scots Worth in Right Subsection commencing 5 p.m.... Companies took up the line as held from N/2W - N/5. "A" in area N. and S. of SOUTHERN SAP. Support Line was held	

WAR DIARY or INTELLIGENCE SUMMARY

Army Form C. 2118.

Place	Date	Hour	Summary of Events and Information	Remarks and references to Appendices
TRENCHES	7/2/16		N. of VERDUN ALLEY and between HAY ALLEY and HOLLY LANE. Hostile artillery was quiet about 4 pm. they came over Enemy made a small bombing attack on SAP 45 time. Machine Guns fired and were full prepared for some in afternoon. About 40 Rifle Grenades were destroyed. We threw over trench. Casualties NIL. D/o+p/ About 20 of which landed in enemy's	
TRENCHES	8/2/16		Bn. on Right Subsection. HULLUCH SECTION. General repair of the trench carried on. Construction of new bays in support trench completed. Support trench carried on. Our front and support line were shelled slightly during the evening. Our "sniper" posts in a tree, maintained active sniping and their Rifle Grenades two fatile exploded German Saps on our front, were much activity was being carried on by the enemy, and which were suspected of being intended for a "sap" or "flammenwerfer" attack. Patrol from "D" Coy. reported a sap believed to be newly made and my narrow and shallow, with no ladders under or about 10 to 15 yards long and near the 15th Infantry Base, and were later to C.O. to the ranks signed from Cape. E. Blow Completed a course of instruction in Lewis Machine guns. 2nd/L6334 L/Cpl. E. Blow Completed a course of instruction in Lewis Machine Gun.	

Army Form C. 2118.

WAR DIARY
or
INTELLIGENCE SUMMARY
(Erase heading not required.)

Instructions regarding War Diaries and Intelligence Summaries are contained in F. S. Regs., Part II. and the Staff Manual respectively. Title Pages will be prepared in manuscript.

Place	Date	Hour	Summary of Events and Information	Remarks and references to Appendices
TRENCHES	9/2/16		Battalion in RIGHT SUB-SECTION, HULLUCH SECTION. Enemy artillery active. Enemy infantry schools of work. Enemy and Rifle Grenade throwing active from our sides. Work was carried on repairing trenches. Our trops were instructed in Support line 30 yards of wire strengthened north of SOUTHERN SAP and about 100 yards of wire were put up in a support line. Pamphlet No S.S. 388 "Defensive measures against Enemy attacks" issued to Companies. 5 O.R. wounded. Casualties 3 O.R. wounded. Rylands	
	10/2/16		Batt in RIGHT SUBSECTION. HULLUCH SECTION. Enemy shelled trenches about 7 a.m. Casualties 5 O.R. Shrapnel wounds. Latter was relieved in RIGHT SUBSECTION by 1/4 Black Watch & went into FAUQUISSART - NEUVE-CHAPELLE SECTION where at 1 p.m. at half-an-hours notice, and had the role of conducting further offensive operations, small local counter attacks by Battalion in the Trenches fall in the event of an enemy counter attack. At the "A" Brigade bombing School ^ N.E. 4 O.R. were wounded through the accidental bursting of a hand grenade. Batt HD QUARTER & 6 Coy of 15th Division. On 8/6 of this date instructions "See alert" when the word is from S.S.F - E - and N.E. Special precautions are ordered for maintaining such alertness in a state of efficiency, and for posting additional sentries to cover men on trellis and in dug-outs. Staff	

WAR DIARY
or
INTELLIGENCE SUMMARY

Army Form C. 2118.

Place	Date	Hour	Summary of Events and Information	Remarks and references to Appendices
PHILOSOPHE	11/2/16		On in Brigade reserve in PHILOSOPHE. Party of 700 men employed clearing reserve trenches, also parties employed in general old silence to LE RUTOIRE ALLEY in VERMELLES in relief of a Rifle Bde. on night of 13-14/4/16. Capt. J.G. Myles rejoined the Battalion for duty and was posted to "B" Coy taking over Command. "A" Coy and no 8/9396 Pte H.J. Burot 5/6022 Sgt R.K. Hancock "C" Coy are afters as selected to attend a Course at the Cadet School, assembling 26th April 1916. DSRP	

Army Form C. 2118

WAR DIARY
or
INTELLIGENCE SUMMARY
[Erase heading not required]

Instructions regarding War Diaries and Intelligence Summaries are in F.S. Regs, Part II and the Staff Manual respectively. Title pages will be prepared in manuscript.

Place	Date Hour	Summary of Events and Information	Remarks & References to Appendices
PHILOSOPHE	11/2/16	Bn. in Brigade Reserve at PHILOSOPHE. Working parties. A new Bridge of 44 Mess.	
	12/2/16	Billeting parties sent to NOEUX-LES-MINES.	Staff
		Bn. moved to billets & ROUTE NATIONALE NOEUX-LES-MINES.	Staff
	14/2/16	Bn. in Divisional Reserve NOEUX-LES-MINES.	
		Training carried on from 9.30 am to 12.30 pm under Coy. Commanders — Squad Drill extd. order.	
		Reports forwarded. Capt. Ian Andrews and Porter Helmet Drill Still.	Staff
	15/2/16	B.Z. at NOEUX-LES-MINES. Day devoted to cleaning at Divisional baths.	Staff
	16/2/16	Bn. at NOEUX-LES-MINES. Training under Coy. Arrangements.	Staff
	17/2/16 1.15 pm	Bn. moved to billets in PHILOSOPHE. C.R.A.B. Corps. Bn. arrived at PHILOSOPHE to be at the disposal of 45th Inf. Bde. for tactical purposes.	
		Advance — Order of March S.E. of LEVER CROSSING. Reclothing and carrying parties for R.E. found at night.	Staff
	18/2/16	Bn. in billets at PHILOSOPHE at disposal of 45th Inf. Bde. Pushing out caring parties Staff	
	19/2/16 6 am	Advance parties left to take over trench sector from 11th R.S.F. Highlanders on Right.	

WAR DIARY
or
INTELLIGENCE SUMMARY.
[Erase heading not required]

Army Form C. 2118

Instructions regarding War Diaries and Intelligence Summaries are in F.S. Regs, Part II and the Staff Manual respectively. Title pages will be prepared in manuscript.

Place	Date	Hour	Summary of Events and Information	Remarks + References to Appendices
			Sub-section PITS and BIS Cotton	
		1pm	B. left level crossing PHILOSOPHE between LENS ROAD and BRENAY —	
			BENIFONTAINE to relieve 11th A.I. Bn.	
			Line was taken over by Stafford Bn. as follows: —	
			Front line — "B" Coy Right "C" Coy Left	
			Support — "D" Coy	
			Village in LOOS — "A" Coy. B	

Reference 1/10,000 Trench Map 36° N.W.3.
Edition 6.

Army Form C. 2118

WAR DIARY
OR
INTELLIGENCE SUMMARY
[Erase heading not required]

Instructions regarding War Diaries and Intelligence Summaries are in F.S. Regs., Part II. and the Staff Manual respectively. Title pages will be prepared in manuscript.

Place	Date	Hour	Summary of Events and Information	Remarks and References to Appendices
			The Bn. first notified from the LOOS - ST-LAURENT ROAD (reserve) to ENGLISH ALLEY (in reserve) — Relief was completed about mid-night. 1 man evacuated to Hospital. Fresh names in two file section replaced by men of "A" & "B" Coys. Tattoo.	DWM
TRENCHES	20/9/16		Bn. in RIGHT SUBSECTION PUITS XIV BIS SECTION. Enemy artillery was very quiet. Our machine guns fired between 600 and 700 rounds. Our German working parties. Rifles claimed a hit. Our casualties 1 man killed and two wounded. Two men evacuated to Hospital.	DWM
"	21/9/16		Bn. in RIGHT SUBSECTION PUITS XIV BIS SECTION. Rebel artillery bombarded German front and support lines and caused Enfilade damage to our lines. Shells fell into our and about our own trenches. Work carried on repairing front and support lines and deepening GORDON ALLEY. Our casualties were 1 O.R. wounded. 17 O.R. proceeded leave to U.K.	DWM

WAR DIARY
or
INTELLIGENCE SUMMARY
(Erase heading not required.)

Army Form C. 2118.

Place	Date	Hour	Summary of Events and Information	Remarks and references to Appendices
TRENCHES	22/7/16		Bn. in RIGHT SUB-SECTION PUITS XIV BIS SECTION. Weather bad. Rain and sleet and cold. Enemy was quiet between 6 p.m. and 9 p.m. They sent on some rifle grenades. Enemy was carried on at enemy working parties and 3 hits claimed. NOR carried on in fire and support trenches and in GORDON ALLEY. Casualties NIL. During the day was fatal to 44th Machine Gun Cy. The Cy. had one machine gun in our line in old Reserve trench N of GORDON ALLEY under 2/Lt Wright. [DIARY]	
"	23/7/16		Bn. in RIGHT SUB-SECTION PUITS XIV BIS SECTION. Weather cold and frosty. Front quiet. At night they were working on their saps, and was very quiet but demonstrative. We threw over Rifle Grenades. On Enfer Lit three bombard. BOYAU ROPIER between BLACK WATCH ALLEY and SEAFORTH ALLEY was deepened. Support trench SEAFORTH ALLEY. NOR was carried on in Headquarters Observation Post. Casualties for the day 1 O.R. wounded by enemy Rifle Grenade. Pvt. J.R. transferred to Ireland for munition work as shewn off the sheet.	

Army Form C. 2118.

WAR DIARY or INTELLIGENCE SUMMARY

Army Form C. 2118.

Place	Date	Hour	Summary of Events and Information	Remarks and references to Appendices
TRENCHES.	17/1/16		On the RIGHT SUBSECTION. PUITS XIV BIS SECTION. Heavy Artillery shell communication between our Suffolk trenches at fields at LOOS. The there was about 75 Rifle Grenades, sent in Suffolk trenches left in front again. BLACK WATCH RELIEF Leeloos out Lodged. Casualties. 16? Corder 6260 Contagues following:- "The following schedule from the Adjutant to the London Gazette dated 16/9/16 is published for information." Leafeth Appendices (See- Rue Suff.) "The Duke of Albany's" Lieut. (now Lieut) Jack Holmes to be Temp Capt. dates 30. 9. 15. " W. J. Taylor " " 26. 9. 15. " John E. Smith " " 30. 9. 15. " Hunt " " " Kent " 30. 9. 15. " Percy W. Shaw " " 30. 9. 15. " L. G. Snell " " 30. 9. 15. " F. J. Murray " " 30. 9. 15. " D. R. Ferguson " " 19. 1. 16.	

WAR DIARY or INTELLIGENCE SUMMARY

Army Form C. 2118.

Place	Date	Hour	Summary of Events and Information	Remarks and references to Appendices
TRENCHES	15/01/16		**Br. in RIGHT SUB-SECTION. PUITS XIV BIS SECTION.** Patrol went out at 3.45 a.m. to reconnoitre towards our right. Two patrols took place in enemy trenches and so found whatever was being done. One was 20 signs of any new tape or digging out. Pts. 4.40 a.m. Sag. Spr. and Patrol were Yorkshire before enemy's machine gun fire. Patrol got safely back. Rifts. Several shots of their new trench rifle rifles being their lines. War-others on fire and suffered trenches. Scots ALLEY defences. Work carried on rearparapets, observation Post. Gaullier. — Sy R.E. Rain slight. Wounded when firing 2 Lentron L/C Bemjh. All became asleep this day except in special circumstances until further notice. J Infantier received 9 o.R. invalided to England. Jr W. Pt. The Largest Bn. closed in to support and fell back to SCOTS ALLEY (Speed Ave.) 1st. Sask ave. is the front.	
TRENCHES	16/01/16		**Br. in RIGHT SUB-SECTION. PUITS XIV BIS SECTION.** Enemy quiet. Our trips active. Enemy snr. fire fired at enemy working parties in early morning. Bomb Stores Ordnance Front Suffolk from kept in repair. SCOTS ALLEY. Casualties NIL JrWR	

Army Form C 2118.

Instructions regarding
War Diaries and Intelligence
Summaries are in F.S. Regs. Part II
and the Staff Manual respectively.
Title pages will be prepared in
manuscript.

WAR DIARY
or
INTELLIGENCE SUMMARY
(erase heading not required)

Place	Date	Hour	Summary of Events and Information	Remarks and references to Appendices
TRENCHES	18/2/16		BN. IN RIGHT SUB-SECTION PUITS 13/15 SECTION. BN IN LOOS was shelled by the enemy with medium H.E. from about 5 to 5.45 a.m. So far as troops are concerned, enemy were inactive. No fire on front and support trenches, in BLACK WATCH ALLEY and SCOTS ALLEY. Casualties NIL. C.O.R. reports invalided to hospital on different dates.	D.v.H.
TRENCHES	19/2/16		BN. IN RIGHT SUB-SECTION PUITS XIV B/5 SECTION. Enemy shelling of LOOS. Casualties NIL. Enemy quiet. Usual San Fan. 9th Cleofeith who were relieved by 1" Cameron's Bn evening of 20th and moved into Engine support in 10a Avenue into the. 1st HeadQuarters at G. 23. B. 5. 5. Working party of 50 men under Lt Bretton were left in LOOS to work on new Reserve trench under R.E. orders. to rejoin that Bn after trench relief was very slow. Enemy were exceptionally quiet at period of relief.	D.v.H.
TRENCHES	20/2/16		BN. in Support PUITS XIV B/5 SECTION. One man slightly wounded with shrapnel.	D.v.H.

www.ingramcontent.com/pod-product-compliance
Lightning Source LLC
Chambersburg PA
CBHW081427160426
43193CB00013B/2214